You Can't Tell Anyone

Corinna Yeager

Dedication

To my only daughter, Maryl: your birth has given me the will to live, survive, thrive, and realize what it means to be loved.

I love you.

Contents

Acknowledgments	7
Chapter One	9
Ninoy Aquino International Airport—October 1988	
Chapter Two	17
Confidential Informant (CI)	
Chapter Three	31
Those First U.S. Days	
"Seeking Approval"	
"My Grandma Annie"	
Chapter Four	41
Quitting Was Not an Option Anymore	
"I Want My Mom!"	
Chapter Five	55
Time to Hide	
"Papa Stay …"	
Chapter Six	69
Maryl Arrives	
"Mary Magdalene"	
Chapter Seven	79
Life in the United States	
"My Sweet Maryl"	
Chapter Eight	91
A Good Christmas, After All	
"An Indecent Woman"	
Chapter Nine	107
Run As Fast As You Can	
"Nowhere to Go"	
Chapter Ten	129
Working Out My Faith	
Epilogue	145
2016: Nothing Lasts Forever	

Acknowledgments

I would like to thank:

My friend Sherry Reeve for encouraging me to write my story. Thank you for believing in me.

My husband, Mark, who loves Maryl and me unconditionally.

My son-in-law, Dale Becker, who always believed in me. You are the son I never had.

My best friend, Mary Rose, and her family. I will always love you.

Zeli Coffee Bar in La Cañada. Thank you for the ambiance of your coffee house, and for these people who make the best coffee. The most wonderful environment allowed me to write my book in peace.

Chapter One

Ninoy Aquino International Airport

October 1988

My heart was pounding so fast it felt like it was going to burst out of my chest. I was wearing an expensive ensemble carefully planned two weeks before—white silk pants, a striped, long-sleeved shirt, and stiletto shoes that I could barely walk on. Thankfully, my best friend's mother trusted me to borrow some of her precious jewelry to adorn myself; I was, after all, posing as a businesswoman. Walking inside the airport, trying to pretend I was familiar with it, was nerve-wracking; I was completely lost and clueless. There were 10 of us being smuggled out of the country that day, but the rest of the group was dressed in jeans and T-shirts. I thought someone had tipped me off, but now that I live in the United States and have traveled extensively, I realize my entire attire back then was literally screaming for attention. It was almost as if I wore a huge sign that said, "I am an illegal alien trying to pose as a businesswoman. Come and get me." If I were indeed a businesswoman, I would have possessed a first-class or business-class ticket. Now I would dress casually to travel. If I really were an experienced traveler, my face would look confident, not rigid and terrified. My hair was so stiff that day with hairspray, not even a typhoon would move it. Unfortunately, I had paid a lot of money for my hair and makeup. Everything about my appearance that night didn't make sense. It was all horribly wrong.

My coach wasn't very smart. I literally would have done a better job if I were in the business of smuggling "illegal aliens." Without a doubt, attention to all detail was missing! As I slowly walked toward the custom booth, I felt like everyone was staring at me. It seemed like an eternity before I finally reached the man in the tiny booth who managed to look straight through me. He immediately asked me, "Where are you going?" I responded, "To the United States." I should have just said "the U.S.," which would have been less obvious. While closely examining my passport, he proceeded to ask me another question: "What are you going to do there?" "Business trip," I said, trying to sound more confident than I felt. His eyes never left my passport as he asked, "Where did you get your passport?" "At the U.S. Embassy," I retorted.

By this time I could feel my fear escalate, but I tried to stay focused. When I am frightened, I get very numb. It was pretty obvious to me that the officer was having a private "eye" conversation with the gentleman next to him—another immigration officer. He finally said, "Wait here." When he walked away, I knew I was a goner. I waited, paralyzed, until he came back and asked me to follow him. Neither of us spoke as I was led to an office that had a big brown desk with a huge picture of the Philippine President above it. There were two coffee tables in between. I noticed that the room was well lit as Col. Rodriguez, the Immigration Consul, walked in and sat down. He had the first friendly face I had seen and didn't beat around the bush. "Your passport is fake, and I need to know where you got it." I didn't say anything. He just stared at me until he finally turned to the other man in the room and said, "Are they coming?" The man simply nodded.

A few minutes later, two American men walked in the room. One was Agent Douglas Forman, a U.S. Immigration Attaché. He looked very tough and serious. The men were whispering to each other for a little while before Forman pulled a chair across from mine and demanded, "I need to know where you got this passport!" I continued to sit there silently. Raising his voice he said, "Did you know that you can go to jail for this?" My mind was racing because the agency told me that if I got caught, no matter what, never to lead the immigration officers to them or they would never be able to send me back for a second try. The price was $5,000 per person with their personal guarantee that they would keep trying to send me until I made it through customs. Of course, they made it very clear that this would all be voided if I got caught and spoke to anyone. Under no circumstance was I to disclose any information at any time.

In 1988, a U.S. dollar was equivalent to 60.00 Filipino pesos. That was an incredible amount of money for me. I literally had to sell everything I owned. I even cashed in on my daughter Maryl's CD to raise all the money that I needed. I had no desire to throw away my last chance to give my daughter a better life. As I waited, I kept a "poker face" and tried to look tough and unaffected. I must have been somewhat successful because Forman actually left the room and was gone for about 15 minutes. When he came back, he sat down slowly, intently staring at me, and said, "I ran your name on our database and found out you have a pending petition from your father in the U.S. Because of what you have done, you will never be allowed to step foot in the States, ever!" Although my face stayed unchanged, when I heard that statement, my heart sank.

Little did these men know, I had been training all my life for this type of situation. I was skilled at hiding my feelings. In fact, not showing my emotions was my forte. After his statement, I was even more convinced to not say anything, no matter what. Clearly, I now stood to lose everything and not gain a thing. Evidently, he didn't realize the full impact of his statement because had he known, he would never have mentioned this. Frustrated and exhausted, Forman finally looked at Col. Rodriguez, who had kept silent during the entire interrogation. For some reason I really liked him and actually thought he felt kind of sorry for me. When Forman left the room, Col. Rodriguez said, "You should just tell them so they will leave you alone. Otherwise you are going to be in jail." I told him I wanted to talk to him privately, so he sent the other men outside.

When the door shut, I began to explain my story to him. Because I was a single mother of a 3-year-old girl, my dream was to go to the United States in order to give my daughter a better life. It was the only place I knew where people wouldn't see you as a prostitute and judge you for your mistake. I explained to him that this was my last chance to change the course of my life. At this point, the only thing I had to help me was the agency, and I couldn't give the officers that information because I would lose everything I had been working for. Unfortunately, for the first time in my life, I literally felt I had no alternate plan.

Col. Rodriguez was sympathetic and said, "What if you give them the names in return for not going to jail?" He continued to explain that they had been following this case for quite a while yet had not had a break up to this point. After thinking about it for a few minutes, I found my leverage. "Look," I said, "I will turn these guys over to you in exchange for your word that you will allow me to live in the States legally with my daughter." Col. Rodriguez thought this was a brilliant idea, so he called Forman back into the room and told him my proposal. After Forman thought about it for a while, he asked, "Do you think you can get me copies of the papers he has filed in his office?" "I can get you whatever you want. I know his schedule thoroughly. I know when he comes in and leaves the office," I said with confidence and a newfound hope in my heart. I could tell this information caught Forman's attention. Once again, he got up and left the room.

When he came back inside, he paced the room before he sat back down and asked me, "What instructions were given to you, in the event you got caught?" I responded, "I am not supposed to show up in the office until everything has cooled off for two days or so. Then I can go back to prepare for a second attempt. But we have to wait for three weeks to a month to schedule the actual departure." Immediately, I could sense that Forman and the other officer realized the value that I would bring to their operation. I later found out that this case was called "Mabuhay." In English, this means, "long live." To this day, I have no idea what the relationship of the operation's name is to the case. I was intercepted around 6:00 p.m. The interrogation lasted until 11:00 p.m. Shortly after everyone finally agreed that I would work as an Immigration and Naturalization Service (INS) Confidential Informant (CI) for Operation Mabuhay, Forman was a lot more relaxed and even managed to act a bit more civil toward me. He started to discuss their strategy. Before he could go much further, however, I interrupted him, saying, "Isn't there some sort of contract I have to sign to seal our agreement? It is very possible for the INS to deny this deal when you get the desired information. What will happen to my daughter and me then?" Although I was polite, my voice was stern as I proceeded to say, "I would like to be able to live in the U.S. legally with my daughter and wait for my father's petition to come through instead of waiting it out here in the Philippines." I could have sworn I saw a smile in the corner of Col. Rodriguez's mouth. I think he thought, *Well, good for you.* I knew what it would take to complete the task. I was about to risk my life. Of course I was afraid, but it was my last chance so I had no other option left but to go for it.

Forman drew up the paperwork, and we signed it. I was given detailed instructions before they released me. My first instruction was that I was not allowed to communicate with my family. Absolutely NO ONE in my family—not my mother or my only sister—was to know about my contract; I couldn't tell anyone! I would be staying in the Philippines until I could get enough information to convict Manuel (the crook's accomplice). The only person I was allowed to tell about my situation was my best friend's family—the Santos family. I thank God in heaven because it gave me an opportunity to see my daughter, Maryl, and spend a little more time with her before I had to leave the Philippines for good. I don't remember sleeping that night, but I distinctly remember the next morning when I was taken back to see Maryl. Understandably, the Santoses were very surprised to see me. I was glad Forman was with me and helped me explain to them the sensitivity of the situation. Col. Santos was totally willing to help support the success of the mission. He was obviously familiar with this kind of situation.

They felt badly for me when they realized the gravity of what I had just gone through. Despite feeling very tired and exhausted, I was thrilled to see my little girl. If things hadn't shifted just the night before, the next time I would have been allowed to see her would have been after at least five or more years in jail and possibly never. Maryl was only 3 years old and didn't really comprehend what was happening. When I saw her, I hugged her and never wanted to let go before I finally kissed her. She was not surprised to see me. Honestly, it was just like any other day to her. For me, it was reassuring to have my daughter in my arms once more, even if for only a few more weeks.

Chapter Two

Confidential Informant (CI)

My work as a confidential informant (the term INS used to address people who work for them as undercover agents) literally began the very next day. My first assignment was to go back to the office and tell Manuel I had been intercepted. It was critical for me to play the part very well. As I walked into his office, I suddenly felt fear creep up inside me. What a relief to realize I was there quite early and Manuel had not yet arrived. The secretary was the only one there. I don't think she fully realized what type of people she was working for, nor did she seem to have a clue why I was there that morning. This was such a profound relief to me when I sat down by her desk. "Where's Manuel this morning?" I inquired in a relaxed manner. "He wasn't supposed to be in until 10:30 this morning," she casually responded. I glanced at the clock; it said 8:30 a.m. I was unmistakably early. While I waited, my eyes scanned the room, carefully studying where the files were located. Initially I tried to have small insignificant conversations with the woman to pass the time, but this was short-lived. My first opportunity finally came when she said, "Hey, can you answer the phone for me when it rings? I need to go to the comfort room." (That is the word for "restroom" in the Philippines.)

"Absolutely!" I barely heard myself respond because my heart was pounding loudly. The restroom was located only 10 feet away, but the hallway curved a bit and made it incredibly difficult to see from the office, especially by the filing cabinet. As soon as the secretary got up, I waited for her to make that curve; then I quickly but quietly went to the designated green filing cabinet. I was primarily looking for the list of the illegal immigrants' names. However, while I was looking through the files, I found additional documents that I knew would make Forman happy. I needed to prove to him that I was "good for it." Without hesitation, I quickly took the file and inserted it in my huge purse. Fortunately, I normally carried a large purse so it didn't seem to raise any suspicions. After only about 15 minutes at the most, she came back and asked, "Did the phone ring at all?" I innocently replied, "Nope, it was completely quiet."

Finally around 11:00 a.m., Manuel walked in. He led me into his private office. Although there was no noticeable expression on his face, I felt like his eyes were piercing right through me. I couldn't help but wonder the whole time, *Does he know? What if he knows and is just waiting for me to admit what I am doing?* As soon as the door shut, I started to talk: "I was intercepted last night, and it was horrible!" He sat down and looked right at me: "Tell me exactly what happened." I went over the rehearsed edited version of what took place at the airport. Much to my surprise, Manuel didn't seem a bit suspicious.

My story must have been convincing because he gave me the impression that he was totally satisfied. There was a well of tears that came out of my eyes as I dramatically told him my "own version" of what had happened that night. What he didn't know was that my tears were really induced by the fear and nervousness I was feeling while I was fabricating my story. When I finally finished, he said, "I am sorry that you had to go through all that. But I am very pleased that you didn't lead anyone back to us. Now we can proceed as soon as possible to work on your second attempt and get you into the States." I immediately fired a barrage of several questions: "Don't you think they are going to recognize me? They took my passport, and I was using my real name. Now am I going to have to use a different name? Will I still pose as a businesswoman? Shouldn't we try a different approach this time? I don't want to go through what I went through last night, so we have to make sure it's a better story this time. Plus, how long will it actually be before I get to try and leave again?"

There really was a reason for all of my questions. These were the questions I needed answered to provide the necessary information for Forman. And most important, he wanted to know the departure date of my second try. Forman had explained to me the procedure and paperwork that needed to be done, the "leg work" so to speak, in order to expedite the whole process. The first thing necessary was the approved I-512 Form. This document is the Authorization for

Advance Parole of an Alien into the United States. In layman's terms, this meant I could stay in the United States legally but with the understanding that I am at the U.S. Immigration's beck and call. Bottom line, they would "own me" until my father's legal petition, for me being a daughter of a citizen, was approved. This was about a five- to eight-year process. It would also mean that I would be able to get a job, a driver's license, and whatever other legal document I sought after to support myself in the United States. Basically, I would get to blend in. I was very grateful for this part of the deal, but I couldn't get a job until we completed the Mabuhay case.

"In two weeks you get to go again," Manuel answered me. "You will need to come here every day before then so we can practice and go over your training again," he added. After about an hour's worth of conversation, Manuel decided I should go home and take a rest so that I would be fresh for my training the next day. Needless to say, I was thrilled to be released. As I shut the door, I wanted nothing more than to run out of there, which would have been far too obvious. Instead, I forced myself to walk normally. All I could see in front of me was the door leading to my freedom. I wanted to grab that door-knob and then run for my life. As I walked past the secretary, I gave her a nice, reassuring smile and told her I would see her the next day. There were quite a few people in the waiting room by this time, and they all looked anxious.

When I left the building, I hailed a cab to go meet with Forman. Although I don't remember where we met, I can remember how excited and impressed he was when I pulled out the documents I had just retrieved from the green filing cabinet. In addition to what he asked for, I gave him very crucial evidence for the case. We spent a little time discussing my conversation with Manuel. Forman wanted to make sure Manuel did not have any clue about what we were doing. That day I knew Forman realized that I was not just the "usual" CI the INS had worked with in the past. Unquestionably, I knew that I had proved myself to him as someone with a disciplined work ethic.

More important, I had just made myself indispensable to his case. For the next two weeks, this process consumed my life. When I wasn't busy with my work, I spent time with Maryl and Stella (my best friend). Stella and her parents were the only people I could contact.

As the day of my departure drew closer, I found myself getting so anxious that I felt sick to my stomach. I had lost my appetite and felt very light-headed most of the time. There were days that seemed completely cloudy and were simply a blur. I remember staring at Maryl often, wondering if I would ever be able to see her again and if the U.S. Immigration would really fulfill their end of the bargain. I didn't sleep very much, and I weighed 109 pounds. I intensely missed my only sister and not being able to talk with her. I worried about her so much because I had always felt like I was her big sister (despite the 11-month difference between us). She and I had been through a lot of difficulties during our lives, and I longed to be with her but couldn't even call her anymore. I knew by now she was wondering what had happened to me. I even missed my nephew and niece.

October 24, 1988, was the scheduled day of my departure to the United States. My flight was leaving at 6:00 p.m. The day before, Forman confirmed we had everything we needed to "nail" Manuel. I was finally leaving to meet the mastermind who resided in the United States. I could barely believe that the next phase of my job and my new life would start as soon as I landed at Los Angeles International Airport. Essentially, a man named Victor (the brains of the operation) was picking me up at the airport. I knew very little about this man, but what I did know was definitely enough to stir in me a strong fear for my safety and even my life. Victor was an ex-high-ranking military man who had previously been with the Philippine military government. He had been smuggling illegal aliens for the past five years. Apparently, as many as 20 illegal migrants were departing every week, and the fee was $5,000 per person. That was obviously a good deal of money, so the stakes were quite high.

It is difficult for me to recall with clarity what happened the day of my departure. I do remember some bits and pieces. I know I sat on a rocking chair by Stella's driveway with my poodle Lionel beside me. Somehow I think he knew he would never see me again. And he was crying. He was a little over 3 years old and used to sleep with me before Maryl was born. I got him when I was about 5 months pregnant. He would always sit with me and managed to follow me wherever I went. I kissed him and said goodbye. I was so upset that I couldn't stop bawling while I held him. Maryl was taking her usual three-hour daily nap. It must have been around noon. I probably sat on that chair for about two hours staring blankly. I was wearing a pair of faded blue jeans and a dark polo shirt with a collar. This outfit was a complete contrast from my previous attire as a businesswoman.

I had also decided to cut my hair very short to disguise myself because it was very long during my initial effort to leave the Philippines. The ironic thing is that I really didn't have to cut it because everyone at the Ninoy Aquino International Airport knew I was on a mission. However, I was convinced it would be a good way to persuade Manuel of my determination to not get intercepted for the second time. I was entirely "in character."

At some point that day, I met with Forman to go over the details of the plan. Once again he reassured me and reminded me to not worry about anything, saying, "Just walk through the terminal and follow your group." He reiterated that the officers had been debriefed about the case so they would not bother me. Even so, Forman said, "They will follow normal procedure, so don't be scared when they ask you a few questions. Try not to let any of your group know what is going on." In addition, we were able to photocopy my $2,500 before I handed it all over to Manuel. This was also part of the deal. According to my contract with Manuel, I would pay Victor the remaining $2,500 when I got to LAX, but only if I was home free. Forman also told me that when I got to LAX he would be there waiting inside the INS office. They planned to pretend to question me so they could buy the time necessary to photocopy the money before I handed it to Victor. Of course, this was all part of the required evidence.

It must have been about two or three o'clock in the afternoon when Stella finally told me we needed to leave for the airport. I knelt down to give Maryl one more hug, and I couldn't stop kissing her. What hurt me the most was that she didn't have any idea what was about to happen. She had a puzzled look on her innocent little face, and I think she honestly thought I was just going away, which I did every day and would return as usual in the evening. She was probably wondering why I was hugging her so hard that I nearly choked her. Because she was only 3, I couldn't tell her anything because I knew she wouldn't understand. I remember I kept saying, "Maryl, promise me you won't forget Mommy. I love you so much. You and Tita Stella will follow me very shortly, okay?" And she naively replied, "Okay, Mommy."

Even though I longed for her to say more things to me before I left, that was the extent of our goodbye. I yearned to hear her say that she loved me and would miss me. Actually, I think I was kind of hoping she would be a little sad that I was leaving her, but in her world, it was just another day no different from any other. When Stella and I pulled away to drive to the airport, my heart literally felt like it was broken. Maryl was with us in the car. Lionel was crying loudly as he ran frantically after our car. I couldn't even bear to watch.

The drive seemed to pass all too quickly. It seemed like we got there in about 10 minutes, and I didn't even talk at all during the drive. By this time I was feeling the full gamut of emotions. It was heartbreaking to leave behind my daughter, my dog, and my sister. In reality, I was very scared for my life, and I didn't know what to expect. Victor's reputation really frightened me. Finally, we arrived at the airport, and I got out of the car. All I had was one big suitcase. In it were Maryl's pictures, along with the one I carried in my wallet. I embraced Stella and thanked her for loving Maryl and looking after her. I gave Maryl one more hug, but I had to turn away very quickly, because I felt like I was going to die without her. We had never been separated before, and I wasn't prepared for the heartache. When I turned back around to look, they were already gone. As I approached the first window where you get asked your destination, I couldn't feel emotions anymore. I wasn't scared or sad, just completely numb. My eyes were already burning and swollen. The officer asked me, "Where are you going?" This time I responded, "Sa U.S. po." This meant "the U.S." in my native language. I passed through three security windows, and no one bothered me. I simply felt like I was a ghost just slipping through unnoticed. For a moment, I forgot all about my precious daughter, Maryl. I was so caught up with the commotion going on while checking in my bag that I didn't seem to notice anyone around me. For the first time in my 25 years of life, I saw a plane up close. It was huge and would take me on a direct flight from the Philippines to the United States. It was a Philippine Airlines Boeing jet 747 that even had a second floor. In spite of my fear and sadness, I was absolutely fascinated. My designated seat was by an exit window. I considered that a blessing because I had never flown before. I remember thinking to myself, *If anything happens, I am so close to the exit that my chance for survival will be great!*

The flight stewardess was beautiful and friendly. I had a huge screen in front of me, and I thought, *How cool! I get to watch a movie.* I asked the stewardess, "Would it be all right if I looked upstairs? I have never been on a plane." She smiled and graciously said that was fine because we had plenty of time. When I reached the second floor, it was even more beautiful than I had imagined. They had bigger seats, and the aroma of the food permeating through the cabin was amazing. The good smell made me realize I was really hungry. I was enamored with the cart filled with different types of liquor and various desserts even though it wasn't for me; I was just sitting on the couch absorbing everything around me.

After exploring, I went back downstairs and sat in my window seat. Immediately I felt the loneliness creep back inside me. I was staring at the ground thinking to myself, *This time I am really leaving.* Then I started to think about Maryl, and a flood of tears besieged me. A man interrupted my thoughts when he said, "Please excuse me, but I will be placing my bag in the bin above." I said okay as I tried to hide my tear-stained face. This gentleman was very nice and friendly. He was a fellow Filipino and was so excited to go home (to the States). I have no doubt that he noticed I was not feeling well, so he tried to make small talk. I shared with him that it was my first time flying and hence I was really scared. Obviously, I didn't even know what to expect. He tried to assure me it was very safe and told me not to worry.

A few minutes later, the stewardess started her flight announce-ment, asking all of us to take our seats, fasten our seatbelts, and prepare for takeoff. While she explained the safety pamphlet, I did my best to understand her instructions. Although I was clear about the cushion on my seat and the oxygen, when she explained the life vest, I felt completely confused. She confidently described that I was supposed to blow through the tube that supposedly would inflate it. However, I have to say it was unbelievable to me, and I didn't trust its reliability. The vests looked flimsy to me, and it seemed like they were broken. When I analyzed the situation, I thought, *Oh well, the cushion is all I really need.* Just then the plane started to move. Even though I kept hiding my tears from my seatmate, I couldn't control them. I could hear myself calling Maryl's name. As we started to as-cend into the air, I broke down and buried my face in my hands while clutching my handkerchief. I knew there was no turning back now, and I kept crying, "Maryl, my Maryl" under my breath.

I remember the first hour of the flight was a bit bumpy. Once again I started to feel anxious, but the gentleman next to me kept talking. When the plane finally settled down at some point, it wasn't so bad. Actually, after the plane was finally steady, it just felt like I was in the living room of my house. The flight stewardess started to prepare our dinner. I was excited because it was Filipino food.

I can remember having Adobo and rice, my favorite Filipino dish. For some reason, all the activity going on made me feel safe despite some intermittent tiny movements from the plane. I think the fact that people were going up and down the aisle made me feel relief. Surely the plane is not going to crash if they are all up and about, I reasoned to myself.

I think it took almost two hours to simply get us our dinner and clean up afterward. After our meal, we were given blankets, and the lights were turned down. I noticed the passengers around me move with haste. While they were scrambling for seats, I wondered, Now what's happening? I soon realized they were trying to find empty seats in order to make a bed. The passengers were preparing for the 14-hour flight we were about to endure. I didn't have their experience so I got stuck with my couch seat. I must have dozed off for a few minutes but was awakened by a big jolt. This really frightened me, but when I looked around, everyone else was still fast asleep. I tried to calm myself down, but I was so antsy I went up to the flight stewardess to ask her for permission to go upstairs into the first-class section. To my surprise she said, "Sure, it's empty, but you will have to come back down to your seat for your meals. You can't have the first-class food."

The first-class section was amazing because the seats were so much bigger and had movie screens. Unfortunately, it wasn't too long until the plane started to experience severe turbulence again. I was so terrified that I started to feel myself getting light-headed, and my hands were wet with sweat. I felt myself stiffen; I was holding onto the arm of the chair so tightly, I couldn't even move. I felt completely paralyzed. I started to cry again. The stewardess noticed my distress and came up to ask me if I wanted water. She told me my face was pale. I told her I didn't need water, then admitted how terrified I was of the turbulence. I even asked her if we were going to crash. She tried to calm me down by explaining how the plane worked and assured me that turbulence was typical. She took time to give me a detailed account about how the clouds and wind made the plane shake. Then she asked me if I wanted to see the cockpit and meet the pilot. She thought it might help me to see how calm they were. "Okay," I said. So she escorted me to the cockpit, and I met the pilots. It surprised me that there were four of them confined in a tiny room. They took time to shake my hand and assured me everything was normal. This really did help calm me down.

In spite of all their support, the rest of the flight I was fully awake; I never shut my eyes again. And I spent the duration of the flight anticipating more turbulence, which preoccupied me so much that I didn't even think about Maryl at all. That was truly a blessing in disguise. My fear kept me so engrossed that I didn't even long for my child or give any thought to the uncertainty of the life I was about to encounter.

It was around 6:30 p.m. when we landed at LAX. I was physically and emotionally exhausted. I was so worn out I could hardly remember Manuel's instruction, "Don't look for Victor. He will find you." I got off the plane and proceeded to the long line where we had to present our I-94 paper and passport. The rest of my group was way ahead of me. As soon as I handed my passport to the immigration officer, he nodded to a nearby INS officer. This man asked me to follow him and led me to an office that was well lit. Fortunately, the first person I saw in the room was Agent Forman. I wanted to run to him and give him a big hug but knew that wouldn't be professional. I was thrilled and comforted to see a familiar face. Disappointingly, Forman was the only person in the entire Mabuhay operation that I trusted. I found myself always suspicious of anyone else. As a matter of fact, I wouldn't take any orders unless they came directly from him. The time that we spent in the Philippines working together on the case allowed me to see who he really was, and the more I got to know him better, the more apparent his integrity and dedication to his job became. He loved his country and took his job as an Immigration Attaché very seriously. Forman was always professional when conducting business. He looked after me in a special manner and treated me with respect and dignity. What I admired the most was how much he loved his three children and valued his family. I knew he was one of the few from the team who clearly understood why I was willing to risk my life.

Forman gave me a big smile when he saw me and inquired how everything had gone. When he asked me where I was supposed to meet Victor, I told him I didn't know and that I honestly didn't even know what he looked like. I had never met him before, and Manuel had never shown us his picture. Forman assured me not to worry because they had placed a few INS officers in position outside. He reminded me that someone would always follow me. Forman was very grave when he sternly said to me, "Don't look around or act like you are looking for anyone. We are following you 24/7. Just know that, and trust me. You cannot in any way cause Victor to suspect anything, or it will blow this case." As he gave me instructions, I could see people hurriedly trying to photocopy the $2,500 cash I was about to give Victor. They had three machines working simultaneously. Obviously they couldn't keep me very long because Victor would get suspicious. When they finally finished, I walked out from the office alone and headed for the baggage claim area.

As soon as I got my suitcase, I walked straight out the exit. I didn't really know what to do next except to keep making my way out of the airport. Right before I made it to the door that went to the outside passenger pickup area, there was a man waiting nearby who looked straight at me. He didn't smile or frown and stood staring at me. I think he was about 5 feet 8 inches, dark, clean-cut, and wearing blue jeans with a beige-colored light jacket. As I walked toward his direction, the man simply said, "Corinna." When I responded yes, he told me to follow him. Then he walked with me to the parking lot and stopped right in front of a brand-new beige-colored Mercedes-Benz that didn't even have license plates on it yet. As I peered inside, I noticed that two of the people who were with me when we left the

Philippines were sitting in the backseat. There also was a lady sitting in the front passenger seat; her appearance immediately struck me. Basically, the man put my luggage in the trunk and opened the door for me to get in. At this point he merely walked over to the driver's seat, put on his seatbelt, looked in the backseat where we were sitting, and said, "I am Victor."

Victor drove us all straight to McDonald's, and we each ordered some French fries, a hamburger, and a soda. I recall thinking to myself, *We have this back home, but for some reason it sure tasted much better in the United States!* I honestly didn't realize how hungry I was. While we were eating, Victor talked business and gave us the entire schedule. He said he would take me home last because my dad's house was closest to his own (my dad lived in Glendale, California, at the time). Victor instructed all of us to be ready at 10:00 a.m. on Tuesday. We were going to the Department of Motor Vehicles (DMV) to get our California ID. After we had finished our meal and as we started to drive away from the airport, I was looking at the view outside the car window. I couldn't believe I was actually in the United States of America! It felt like it was about 50 degrees outside, and I was freezing (this was in October). I was so used to temperatures in the 90s with 100% humidity. Except for the cold weather, it seemed just like the Philippines to me. I couldn't help thinking, *What's the big deal?* Most people said the United States was so beautiful, but as far as I could see, it was just like driving on Makati Avenue back home.

I think we got to my dad's house somewhere around 11:00 p.m. Victor dropped me off and then disappeared. My dad lived in an apartment back then. I looked for his name on the directory gate at the entrances. As soon as I pressed the buzzer, I heard my stepmother's voice over the speaker, "Come on up."

The last time I had seen my dad, I had been 12 years old. My stepmother opened the door and seemed genuinely pleased to meet me. Unfortunately, that wasn't the case with my dad. When my dad saw me, I immediately felt just like old times. Without any delay, he gave me a look of disdain. Predictably, he didn't manage to say much to me except to ask, with his displeasure apparent, why I had arrived so late that evening. In a way, I guess I really couldn't blame him because he honestly didn't have any idea when I was supposed to arrive. Remember, I couldn't tell anyone or give out any details. So in all fairness to him, he must have been taken by surprise when I was standing in his living room late that evening. My stepbrother was there, and I think he was in junior high at the time. They all had to go to work and school the next day, so my stepmother pulled out the sofa bed and tried to make it comfortable and pleasant for me, giving me a blanket and pillows. Then she showed me around the apartment, paying particular attention to where the restroom was and where any necessary towels or washcloths were located. Right after that, she said we would be able to visit in the morning and excused herself after saying goodnight.

Without hesitation I changed into my pajamas, turned off the lights, and realized it was too quiet. Once I fully comprehended I was not in my own home but in a place that was completely new and foreign to me, I wasn't a bit sleepy anymore. I stood by the window and gazed outside. It was dark enough for me to see the stars, and suddenly I realized how much I missed Maryl. Immediately, my tears flooded, and I tried very hard to be quiet. My heart ached to hold her and kiss her like I did every night before we went to bed together. I opened the window a little bit so I could feel a touch of the breeze. When I closed my eyes, I instantly imagined Maryl was in my arms. I tried to smell the breeze that was coming in, hoping to smell her scent floating through. I tried to hug myself tightly, hoping I could remember how her little body felt against mine. Still, nothing satisfied my longing for her so I resignedly shut the window only to bury my face in the pillow, as I let out sorrowful sobs no one could hear.

Chapter Three

Those First U.S. Days

The next morning, everyone was in a hurry to get to work and school. My stepmom was caring. She managed to make eggs and corned beef for me that morning. I don't think I ate much, but I vividly recall having some coffee. My stepbrother went to school, and my dad went to work. I didn't speak with my dad at all. A logical assumption is that at age 25 I would no longer be scared of him. Unfortunately, I was. All he had to do was give me "the look." It wasn't even that he glared at me. It was really more like a look that screamed of disgust—and a look that stirred up a bunch of memories.

Seeking Approval

🌺

Sadly, I had spent most of my adult life simply trying to please my dad. All I ever wanted was for him to love and accept me. As a little girl, I always wondered why he didn't like me and what I had done wrong. At this point I had almost convinced myself that I was not actually his child—except, I looked exactly like him. In fact, I can remember most of our family members exclaiming, "Oh my, you are definitely the girl version of your dad. Why, you even laugh like him and talk like him. You both have the same sense of humor." Deep inside, I felt so much joy when people said these things to me, because it was the only time in my life when I felt like I truly belonged to him, that I was actually his daughter. The funny thing is that I sincerely loved my dad very much. Essentially, I respected a lot of things about him. And when I was a young girl, I thought my dad was one of the most handsome men I had ever known. My desire was to marry someone who was just like him. What I admired most about my dad were his intelligence and his humor. Indeed, he was really smart.

My dad started his career as a car salesman for Mariwasa Honda in the Philippines. I witnessed firsthand the success he had in his job. I understood at a very young age what success was and had a distinct awareness that the owner of the company liked my dad. I think it was because he was such a loyal employee. And I know the feelings were mutual because the owner favored him. My dad worked very hard and was an overachiever. He not only did everything he was asked, but he also was always willing to do even more. One of the most important lessons I learned from my dad was to value an excellent work ethic. He often used to say, "Whenever your boss asks you for one, make sure you come back and give him two. And never say no to your boss; always do whatever he/she asks you." I believe this is the reason why I have been one of those fortunate people in the workforce who has always had great relationships with my superiors. Although that begins with my immediate supervisor, it also rolls all the way up to the owner of the company.

Interestingly, when I reflect back upon my childhood memories, it actually sounds like I idolized my dad. I think I was about 10 years old when my mom asked me to get dressed up because we were going to my dad's work. Apparently he hadn't given my mom our monthly allowance yet. She made sure I was wearing something especially nice because my dad would get so upset if I wasn't dressed properly. We took the bus to his office, and when we arrived, my mom sent me up to the eighth floor to see my dad. As I recall, it must have been at least two months since the last time I had seen him. Although I was exceptionally nervous, I also remember how excited I was to see him. I looked especially cute that day, wearing a dark blue dress with my haircut stylishly short. It was one of those few times when my mom simply didn't have time to get our usual haircuts so we looked feminine.

Typically my mom would take my sister and me to a barbershop—yes, a barbershop. A barber instead of a hairdresser would totally butcher my sister's and my hair. This would bring both of us to tears whenever we would leave the shop. I would try to run my fingers behind my ears and there was no hair! Needless to say, because my hair is curly, it made me look like I was a bald boy. Although my sister was lucky because she had beautiful, straight, silky hair, she would end up looking like a little Vietnamese kid too. Even though *we walked in to the barbershop looking like typical girls, when we came out from that place we had the distinct appearance of boys.*

So, when the elevator opened at my dad's office and he was standing in front of me, he sized me up from head to toe. He smiled, and I was ecstatic. I knew he approved of what I was wearing and he liked what he saw. My dad put his arms around me as he guided me from behind. I watched him look into the windows of all the offices. He had this grin on his face. We sort of slowly paraded down the hallway at his work together. When we finally stopped and walked into the vice president's office, my dad proudly said, "This is my youngest daughter. She is the pretty one." I think I had been with him for a little over 40 minutes. He asked me how my mom was doing and then gave me 500 pesos. I gave him a kiss on his cheek, and then off I went. When I took the elevator back downstairs, I felt my shoulders go back and I held up my head much higher than when I had arrived. I could feel a huge smile plastered on my face, and I felt like I was walking on clouds. I have never forgotten that day because it was the last time I remember ever seeing my dad pleased with and proud of me. My dad's expression is forever etched into my memory.

Forman had scheduled an appointment to see me the day before I was to meet with Victor. We went to the U.S. Immigration building located in downtown Los Angeles. The first thing we took care of was getting my fingerprints. Unfortunately, it looked and made me feel like I was a convict being processed for jail. As we made our way to this first section, we passed by some men who were in a glass-enclosed room. When they saw me walk in with Forman, they all started to cheer and made some derogatory remarks accompanied by obscene gestures.

"Just ignore them," Forman told me. When we finished with the fingerprints, he took me to one of the conference rooms. There were already about five gentlemen inside waiting. I was introduced to a man named Agent Jimenez, who was a staggering 6 feet 1 inch daunting Hispanic officer with a very straight face. Just his presence was intimidating to me. Forman informed me that Jimenez was the main man in the U.S. Immigration operations. Even though the Mabuhay case was Forman's, someone had to be in charge of what happened in the United States. Jimenez knew all about the case, specifically Victor the mastermind, and Forman had carefully studied Manuel, the partner back in the Philippines. Then there was Agent Price. He was a 6 feet 2 inches Caucasian gentleman, who seemed much more approachable. Because I am only 5 feet 2 inches, I absolutely looked like a dwarf in the midst of all these men.

During our first debriefing meeting that morning, the immigration officers kept reminding me that my safety came first. Of course, this was partially due to the fact that they had just finished explaining to me that I would be wearing a wire whenever I needed to meet with Victor. They had to record everything we discussed for evidence in this important mission. This team also explained quite clearly that the pictures of Victor dropping off and picking up aliens simply would not be enough to convict him, especially if I was not in the picture with him. It was crucial to make absolutely sure that Victor uttered a few important phrases. In particular, they wanted him to say the exact amount he charged for each person smuggled into the United States and how he planned to smuggle my daughter to be with me. In addition, they needed to hear his strategy to get all people smuggled over and how he intended to get them all official legal documents. Obviously, the officers were very careful and strategic about the whole operation. I knew they were totally invested in this case, but I didn't really understand until that particular meeting the total ramifications of this mission and all that was at stake.

That night when I went home, my dad was totally furious! Without a doubt, he uttered the worst curse words known to man and managed to come up with some of his own. He fiercely accused me of endangering everyone's lives, which meant his entire family. He was especially concerned about the safety of my stepmom, stepbrother, his three sisters, four of his brothers, and my Grandma Annie, who was in her early 70s at that time. During his rage, he informed me that all I had ever brought to him in his life was grief. Then he literally threw me out of his apartment and told me to move to my grandmother's house immediately.

I had to call Victor to give him the address of my new location. I also had to get in touch with Forman to see if he could pick me up and take me to my grandmother's house. When I saw Forman later, he told me that he and Agent Jimenez had a long talk with my dad earlier that day. Forman explained to me that they had to tell my dad what was going on but that he really didn't respond to the information very well. Forman said that my dad was clearly fearful about this whole situation. He expressed his apparent concern, which seemed mostly for his own safety without much regard for my own life.

Grandma Annie lived with my dad's youngest sister. Needless to say, my aunt was unbelievably kind and gracious to extend the same hospitality to me because she was the actual owner of the house. My grandmother simply lived with her. Surprisingly, neither of them asked me to explain why my dad kicked me out of his home, nor did they ask any details about the mission I was working on with U.S. Immigration. Instead, they just took me in, unconditionally. I wondered if either of them knew. I was also very excited to see my first cousin whom I grew up with in the Philippines. I just loved him, and he always had the ability to make me laugh.

That night, however, I couldn't seem to find my sense of humor. In fact, it had been several months since I last laughed. I was feeling physically, emotionally, and mentally exhausted.

Much later when I began to write my story, I started missing my grandma. Sadly, she passed away in 2007. That was very difficult for my whole family because she was almost perfect. I have always been painstakingly referred to as a difficult child. My sister was always considered the good girl. This was one of the reasons why Grandma Annie tended to favor her so much. And my dad was always my grandma's favorite child. In the Philippines, this type of favoritism is the norm. People accept this practice without ever giving it a second thought.

Before I went to bed that night, I prepared for my meeting with Victor. I took the auto-activated mini voice recorder and inserted the tiny cassette tape. Forman asked me to record all of our conversations, and I made sure I had enough blank tapes for this to happen. I placed the tape recorder inside my green bag. This bag had a special kind of zipper that can zip on either side, either to the left or to the right, meeting in the center. My bag also had several little secret compartments. At this point, little did I realize that this very inexpensive bag would soon save my life.

The next morning, I was up earlier than everybody else in the house except for my grandma. Ever since I was a little girl, I can remember her waking up earlier than everyone else. Grandma Annie would go to a Catholic church and attend the first service each day. As soon as she came back home, she prepared breakfast for all of her grandchildren, which was not an easy feat when there were six of us kids in her big house during summer. I didn't realize how much I loved her and had no concept how much I would miss her.

My Grandma Annie

❈

Grandma Annie was one of the most amazing women I have ever known. A few months before she died, God gave me an opportunity to spend some time with her in the hospital. For some reason, my aunt was unable to get away from her work so I eagerly offered to watch my grandma. At this point, she was very frail and falling in and out of consciousness. Grandma was also suffering from dementia so her memory would come and go without warning. I had been sitting beside her hospital bed for about 15 minutes when she opened her eyes wide and inquired, "Who's there?" Without any hesitation, I replied, "It's Corinna, Grandma!"

Grandma was often disoriented, but much to my surprise, she remembered who I was that day in the hospital. She would usually think that I was either my sister or one of my other cousins and refer to me by their names. But on this particular day, it was special because she not only knew me, but also remembered details about my job. She even asked why I didn't go to work that day. I explained to her that my boss was very understanding and had allowed me to visit her.

Because she was thinking with clarity, I took the opportunity and posed questions I have always wanted to ask her since I was little. My first question was, "Grandma, was Grandpa a womanizer?" "Absolutely!" she answered without hesitation and with a smile. So I proceeded to ask her why she stayed with him. She said it was because of her seven children who were very little. She continued, "He made a lot of money and was a very good provider, and that was all I really cared about back then. He came home every night anyway, and there was nothing I could do to stop him."

Then I asked if she remembered the war in the Philippines during the Japanese occupation. I wanted to know how they survived with all those little children. She told me that my grandpa was a coward who was very afraid of the Japanese. Although they had the money to spend during that time, it really didn't matter because pesos didn't have any value. They had to barter and trade to simply get the rice, potatoes, and corn. Meat was especially scarce. She continued to say, "We [my grandma and her neighbors] used to wake up at 2:00 a.m. and would climb on the roofs of houses. When the train started to slow down, we would all jump on the roof and hang on for our dear lives. This was our way to get to town without the Japanese military seeing us. That was how we got food for our families. Then we would come back the same way."

I was so impressed and proud of my grandma. After she told me this incredible story, I said to her, "Grandma, you are, after all, the real Indiana Jones, except maybe I should call you Indiana Jane!" It was great to make her giggle that day; it gave me so much joy to hear *her laugh. Then she asked about my husband because she was quite fond of him and loved him. She told me that she prayed for all of her children and her grandchildren and even their spouses by name every single day. After our time together that day, she went back to sleep. Regrettably, that was my last conversation and final time with her. She died in April of 2007 at the age of 97.*

Chapter Four

Quitting Was Not an Option Anymore

It was about 6:30 a.m. on the morning of my meeting with Victor. The INS van was parked across the street from my grandma's house, hidden between two cars. It looked like one of those vans that you take when you go on a camping trip. They picked me up, and I was taken into an office. I don't recall anymore if it was the immigration office or just a rented office for the operation. When I walked in, I was a bit surprised to see a woman already waiting in the room. I was told, "Corinna, this is Agent Aguilera. She will hook you up with the wire. Tell her where the best place would be. We need to do this quickly because we need to get you back to your grandma's house before Victor shows up."

I didn't really have an opportunity to say anything before Agent Aguilera led me away to another room. She asked me if I could lift up my shirt. I was wearing a very loose, white-and-green-striped sweater. I said yes, but I was honestly a bit embarrassed even though she was very polite. The first thing she did was to take out a tiny microphone. This was probably the same size as a small Bluetooth in the year 2012. Without any hesitation, she clipped it right between my breasts in my cleavage. Then she started to unravel the rest of the wire, which was approximately 2 feet long, and when she got toward the end of it, there was a little black box attached. This box was similar in size to a playing card except that it was kind of bulky and heavy. She next asked me to turn around, and as I did, she pulled on the back of my jeans and inserted the box inside.

As soon as it touched my back, it felt a little bit warm so I commented to her, "It's kind of warm; is that normal?" "Don't worry, it's all right. It does tend to heat up just a little bit so I will place this thick piece of cardboard behind it to protect your back," she calmly replied. As soon as she did this, it felt much better. She checked everything one more time, just to make sure it was fastened securely. She shook it slightly to make sure it wouldn't fall off and then nodded. After that we left the smaller room and went into the other office where we found Agents Jimenez, Price, and Forman waiting.

"Are you all done?" Jimenez inquired. "Yep!" she replied. Then we rushed out of there, almost running with total focus.

As soon as we got into the van, Jimenez turned to me and said, "Listen, we want to remind you that your safety is more important than this case. If at some point you feel you have been compromised, all you have to do is run outside. There are four vans located strategically close for this surveillance. Once you step outside, we won't hesitate to come for you." "Okay...yep, got it," I muttered. Within an hour, we were back at my grandma's house. I walked back upstairs to begin the wait for Victor.

At exactly 9:00 a.m., his Mercedes-Benz pulled up in front of the house. Victor watched me come down the steps as I walked out of my grandma's front door. He didn't even bother to open the car door for me this time. As soon as I climbed into the car, I found the same people who were with me the night we arrived. Once again the strikingly beautiful woman was sitting in the front passenger's seat. I had figured out by this time that she was Victor's girlfriend. An interesting twist was that he had a wife and children in the Philippines. "Hi" was all he said before we drove off. Come to think of it, he never even introduced us passengers to each other. Therefore, I have no idea what their names were.

We drove from Los Angeles to Glendale, California. The DMV was pretty packed by the time we arrived. Victor gave all three of us very clear directions on where we were to go and exactly what he expected us to do, but he didn't go inside with us. By now I had noticed that Victor was truly a pretty sleek kind of guy. Somehow, he managed to keep his distance and didn't really smile or have too much to say. I had also noticed that when he drove he always seemed suspicious, like someone was following him. His eyes darted around very quickly; he continually looked over his shoulder and was always alert. I found myself starting to wonder what division he was in when he served as an officer in the military. Somehow, I wouldn't be a bit surprised if it was in the Intelligence Division because he appeared to be skillful and well-trained and he exemplified extraordinary expertise. He wasn't good-looking, but he carried himself very well. It is mind-boggling to me how he could exude such personality doing what he was doing as a criminal.

Luckily, I was the first one to get everything completed at the DMV. I found myself thinking that I should stand beside Victor and talk to him so the INS officers could take the necessary pictures for their "scrapbook," as I mentally laughed.

However, as soon as I started to walk toward Victor, he came up to me and tried to put his hands around my waist. I was petrified and felt a wave of panic! The microphone black box was on the same side he started to take hold of, so I jumped quickly.

Victor immediately gave me a suspicious look and commented, "My, aren't we a little jumpy this morning?" "Well," I retorted, "I am not used to men touching me, especially around my waist." Even though he didn't say anything, I distinctly felt like he didn't believe me. Victor was much too smart to accept this answer, so I immediately began to think about what I should do next. Despite feeling unsure, I forced myself to stay composed. Just a few minutes later, the two other people from our group started to walk out of the DMV office door. Trying to not be too obvious, I hurriedly rushed ahead of them to the car to strategically position myself by the car door. My concerned thought was that if he knows, then I am actually in much danger. I was willing to jump out of the car simply to save my life. I also realized that my back hip where the gadget was placed in my jeans absolutely had to be against the car door and could not be against a person!

Once again, Victor didn't say much when we started to drive. He didn't even bother to tell us where we were going or give us any hint about what we were going to do next. I realized he did that on purpose because he feared we would talk to others. Honestly, the "unknown" makes me extremely nervous. Yet I knew in my heart God's protective hand was upon me. Just when I literally felt I would pass out from the overwhelming fear, I noticed right beside our car to my right was an undercover INS van. In fact, the driver even gave me the signal to identify them. Needless to say, I was flooded with relief. Ironically, I later learned from Forman that Victor's car was in the middle of the carefully camouflaged INS vans. Unbeknownst to me at that time, we were completely surrounded with a van on the right, one on our left, one in the back, and one in front of our car. Forman said they purposefully made a lot of room to distance their vans from our car and stay out of sight. They had to rotate and move often because Victor was very clever. He was obviously suspicious, and they were concerned he would figure out that someone was following him. At one point Victor even got off the freeway we were on, then went right back on. I later learned from Forman that at this point, the INS officers lost track of Victor for about five miles. I could have used that information earlier, I thought, but then I realized that in this case, ignorance was bliss. All I can tell you is that if I sincerely knew what was going to happen before they recruited me, I certainly would never have agreed to do anything.

We had been on the road for about an hour when I felt the gadget heating up on my back. I started to panic because the Mercedes had leather seats and I was afraid I would not only burn myself but the car seat too! I gathered all my inner strength and very calmly said to Victor, "I need to go to the restroom as soon as you see one, please." Although he didn't say anything, Victor did stop at a quick-stop shop. This was ideal because there were a lot of people around and it was big. Luckily, none of the other ladies in the car had to go in the restroom except me. I ran out of the car as soon as he stopped to pretend that I was dying to go. Truthfully, the running was just out of my complete fear.

When I walked into the restroom, there was only one other lady there who was on her way back out. I was panting and starting to feel faint. Another woman walked in, and she started washing her hands. She smiled at me, and I can't even remember if I smiled back at her.

Then she calmly said, "I think you know my friend." It took me a few seconds to engage, and then I responded, "Which friend would that be?" Without hesitating she said, "Forman." As soon as she said that, I held on to the sink and fought to stop myself from crying. I said to her, "Oh my God! I am so scared! I think he knows. This gadget has burned my back, and you have to get this off now!" She simply said, "Okay." She didn't contradict me or try to change my mind. Instead, she started to remove the gadget very quickly. I told her, "I have to go right now. Tell them to stay close because I think he knows. If I open the window and put my hand out, it means I am in danger or he is about to hurt me." "Will do, good luck," she replied. I thought to myself, *Seriously? Are you kidding me? Good luck? Is that all you can say to me?* In my world she should have said, "Don't do this anymore because your life is probably in danger" and then whisked me away to safety!

I was only in the restroom for about 10 minutes at the most. I tried to pull myself together and started to walk back to the car. Because the gadget was removed from my back, I no longer cared if my seatmate accidentally touched me. We never even took the time to exchange names, and by no means did Victor ever introduce us to each other. I am sure the three of us were all experiencing mixed emotions. We were smuggled into the United States, and none of us knew what was going to happen. We were all thrust into a car with a man of few words who left little reassurance for our future. Personally, I felt very lost. Not only was I unaware of my surroundings, but I also didn't even know where anything was so I couldn't tell if Victor was actually taking us where we were supposed to go. I am sure the other two passengers were homesick too and just as fearful of the unknown as me.

As usual, Victor didn't say one word when I finally got back into the car. We continued to drive in total silence for quite a while. Fortunately, I wasn't too scared during this drive because I now knew for sure the INS vans were all around me. It was just like a scene from the movies. Come to think of it, I don't believe I ever saw a crime drama movie until I arrived in the States.

I Want My Mom!
🌸

I was raised in the Philippines with very little television privileges. I was allowed to watch television for only one hour a day and that was all. The rest of the day, I played with my cousins and read books. Basically, Grandma Lola, who was my mom's mother, and her oldest daughter, raised me. My mom and dad gave me to them to raise when I was only 3 years old. I clearly remember that every Saturday afternoon, my mom would come pick me up so I could go home with her to see my dad and sister. They lived with Grandma Annie, my dad's mother. Where my mom, dad, and sister stayed wasn't exactly a house; it was actually more like an additional room under my grandma's roof. This place had a very tiny living room with only one window. I think they had a little television placed in the center. I honestly don't even remember if there was a couch in there. There was a white crocheted curtain that separated the bedroom from the living room. The floor was always kept very shiny and slippery. My mom used the husk of a coconut to scrub the floor. She would scrub the floor, and I can still recall her saying, "It's good exercise; it will make you sexy."

My bedroom was dark and tiny as well. On these Saturday nights, I shared a single bed with my sister, and we had figured out a way to both fit in the small space. We slept in opposite directions of one another. Her feet were beside my face, and my feet were beside her face as well. Sometimes I would fall out of my bed and then have to climb back up in the middle of the night. Right across from our bed was another bed where my mom and dad slept. Obviously, there wasn't any privacy for them. My dad's eldest brother (he was third of the seven children) lived beside us in a tiny house too. My uncle had two girls who were the same age as my sister and I.

Grandma Annie often said that the reason why my mom and

dad's marriage didn't survive was because they married the same year as my uncle. Grandma said it was truly bad luck to share the same year when you got married. Most Filipino people are very superstitious like my grandma. One day, my uncle's children came out to tell me they were going to Luneta, a place right by the bay. At this time it was very clean, and the public still swam there. People took their children there for recreation and to enjoy a picnic. Because I loved going there, I rushed inside our house to find my dad and tell him the news. He was sitting on a chair so I squeezed myself between his legs, looked him straight in the eye, and while still out of breath from running said, "Dad, let's go to Luneta today!" He said "No," but I was insistent and kept pleading, "Please, Dad, let's go now." I was whining and he kept telling me no.

In desperation I finally stomped my feet and cried, "How come uncle and his children are going? Why can't we go too?" I will never forget the look on my dad's face as he glared at me and yelled, "Why are you jealous? You're jealous? How many times have I told you not to ever, ever get jealous, huh?" Dad left long enough to find a wooden hanger. When he came back, he started hitting me hard while he fumed and repeated those words over and over again. I tried to get away, but it was futile because his grip on me was so tight. I was moving so much trying to free myself from him that I ended up getting hit on several different parts of my body. At some point my mom asked him to stop, and she snatched me away from him. When my uncle asked my dad if they could just take me with them, he emphatically said, "No!" I think my uncle felt really bad for me. I was probably 3 or barely 4 years old.

During this time of my life, I hated when Sunday came because this was the day my mom would take me back to Grandma Lola. I didn't like leaving my parents. I especially loved being with my mom, and I simply adored her. We usually left right after lunch. We would take the jeepney, which is a form of public transportation, because we didn't have our own car back then. Both my dad and my mom had just started their jobs. Every Sunday I would beg my mom not to take me back to my Grandma Lola, but it was to no avail. Mom told me that no one else would take care of me. She let me know that I was a lot more difficult to handle than my sister and reminded me that my aunt and Grandma Annie refused to care for me. No wonder my young heart sank each time we walked away from our little home.

The scenario was always the same. I would cry, and ultimately my mom would have to drag me away. Our travel time was under an hour, and as soon as we would walk into my Grandma Lola's house, I would shape up and gain composure because I was deeply afraid of her. She disliked whining, and unruly behavior was simply not tolerated. My aunt (my mother's eldest sibling) owned the house, and Grandma Lola lived with her. This home had two bedrooms, a big yard, a nice kitchen, and another kitchen outside of the house. Grandma Lola also had a servant named Ellen. My aunt had two children at that time, a boy and a girl. I also truly admired her husband. His love for my aunt was apparent, and he never seemed to care how many people lived in his house. He was a very generous man. My mom's youngest brother and her younger sister also lived with my aunt. There were quite a few people in that house for company, but it never mattered to me because I still wanted to stay with my mom and dad. By the time we would get to their house, I would be completely exhausted. I am assuming most of the exhaustion came from crying all day and the despair of having to leave my family once again.

On one particular night, I devised what I thought to be a brilliant plan. I usually wore a white T-shirt and had shorts with ruffles on the back. My mom sat down by me on the couch. While she was having a very serious talk with my grandma, I pulled the end corner of my white shirt and then I pulled out the end corner of my mom's shirt. I tied our shirts together and made a really strong knot. While I did this, I thought to myself, There is no way you can leave me now without me knowing it! Ha! *After that, I sat there quietly, and for the first time I was actually calm because my mom was "tied to me" after all. According to my little-girl thinking, she was now not going to go anywhere without me.*

I was startled by a voice over my head that said, "Go upstairs; it's bedtime." Grandma's voice broke into my calm delight. I honestly couldn't figure out if I was awake or dreaming. Even when I tried to open my eyes, things still seemed a bit blurry. One of the first things I did was grab the end of my T-shirt. To my utter dismay, the knot was already untied, and my mom was gone! I started to cry, and in between my sobs I kept asking where my mom was. I was so hopeful that she had just gone to the restroom. However, my grandma had a way of bringing one back to reality; she scolded me and didn't even try to console me. I can still clearly hear her stern voice forcefully say, "What is wrong with you today? She picks you up and drops you here every week. You should be used to it by now." I internally screamed "NO! I will never get used to being left here by myself; I want my mom and my dad back!" Of course, I would never dare say such things to my Grandma Lola.

It was almost noon when Victor finally arrived at our destination; I distinctly recall this because the couple, who I assumed owned the house we were at, had prepared a special Filipino dish for us. Even though it had only been days since I left home, the aroma of food familiar to home never smelled so wonderful. In fact, this was the first time I had ever seen Victor smile and interact with the people around him. Victor expressed his anticipation of eating Filipino food and said it had consumed his thoughts during our drive.

In total contrast to Victor, I, on the other hand, was extremely nervous, and my mind wouldn't stop racing. I stood right by the front door, which they left open because the temperature that day was warm. I glanced across the street until I found what I was looking for—the INS van. Somehow I knew in my heart that Victor was just waiting for an opportunity to search my bag. I was acutely aware that I needed to find a way to get rid of the mini-recorder I still had and carried almost the whole time we had traveled. I had to use it to replace the microphone gadget. Seeing Victor let down his guard, the first thing I did was ask the woman of the house where her restroom was located. "Well," she said, "we have two actually. One is on your left, and the other one is upstairs. Feel free to use either one of them." The earlier drive had taken so long that all five of us needed to use the restroom. Yet I didn't need to be in the bathroom for the same reason as everyone else.

I waited for somebody to go in the restroom downstairs to give me the opportunity to use the one upstairs. Sure enough, someone eventually did so I climbed upstairs quickly, found the restroom, and locked myself inside. I didn't have any idea where I should hide the mini-recorder because I would have to be able to retrieve it before we all left. I quickly looked around and decided to use the cupboards that were right in front of me beside the bathroom sink. The cupboards were already full with bath towels. Without hesitating, I took the mini-recorder and my address book, which was filled with all the INS information, and wrapped them completely with one of the hand towels I found in there. Then I pushed all the towels forward, shoved the wrapped mini-recorder and address book underneath, and then pushed the towels neatly back to where they had been originally. I figured this was safer than anywhere else. Bottom line, I couldn't think of any other place. Before leaving the restroom, I washed my face to bring back some color to my cheeks and slowly walked back downstairs.

By the time I got downstairs, everyone else was already eating. I don't really remember if I ate anything or not, but I do know I stood by the front door the entire time with my bag still on my shoulders. Thinking about that day, it probably didn't help me knowing that I couldn't let that bag out of my sight. When everyone finished eating, Victor finally started to explain the plan. I recall thinking to myself, *I sure could use the recorder on this one.* The three of us were to apply for amnesty, which the U.S. government gives to illegal aliens who have lived in the United States for the last 10 years working as farmers.

Victor also stressed the importance for us to get trained and learn to pick grapes. He informed us that we literally had to work on the farm because our hands needed to look like we were actual grape pickers. They could not be soft and supple anymore to pass for migrant workers. All of a sudden it occurred to me why the place we were eating at looked so provincial. I realized we were at a Santa Maria farm and began to understand that the couple who fed us probably owned this farm.

Although my mind was racing, Victor methodically continued to explain that our plan for that day was to drive to the U.S. Immigration office for our preliminary interview. He made it clear that the person who would be interviewing us was an actual immigration officer. Victor encouraged us to not appear nervous. We were told to simply answer all of the officer's questions and were guaranteed that everything would be fine. At this point I grasped more clearly why the U.S. Immigration officers were so devoted to this case. The more I became involved, the more apparent it became that there were many people involved in this complex operation. What made this case so significant was the fact that Victor would actually lead the U.S. Immigration investigators directly to the specific immigration officer who was ultimately responsible for approving the amnesty for all the illegal aliens smuggled into the country by Victor and Manuel. As the pieces fell into place, it all made so much more sense to me. However, it also made me fear Victor so much more as I realized the complexity and intensity of this operation. Is he even afraid to get caught? Where did he find the courage, and how did he ever develop all the resources necessary to put this whole operation together? It was hard to believe he had only been doing this for a few years.

The impact of this realization compelled me to want to make a run for my life. Clearly, that was not by any means an option because

I gave my word and made a deal. I was completely committed to following this operation through; I was chiding myself that I was almost at my objective and soon Maryl would be able to join me. Needless to say, if I quit now, all my time and previous efforts would have gone to waste. There was absolutely no turning back now. Quitting wasn't even an option anymore. I couldn't ever go back to the life I had left behind, and I had no desire to fail Maryl or sabotage my dream for our future. "Time to go, guys," Victor interrupted my thoughts. Without hesitation, everyone headed for the door and again piled into the car. We probably drove for about 30 minutes, but it felt more like an eternity to me.

When we arrived at the Immigration office, Victor once again informed us all that he would not be accompanying us into the office. He repeated his instructions that we were supposed to just follow the signs once inside and any direction they gave us. As the three of us started to get out of the car, Victor stopped me and said vehemently, "Corinna, you don't need to take your purse in there! Go ahead and just leave it in the car." "Oh, okay, it's probably better," I managed to respond. Before I set my purse down on the car seat, I pretended I had to dig out my handkerchief to take inside. Instead of zipping the bag all the way to the right, I zipped the zipper to the middle and carefully left a two-inch gap. I did this intentionally so I would be able to tell if Victor went through my bag while I was inside.

After we got inside the Immigration office, we were directed by the guard to sit and wait for our names to be called. Once my name was called, a Hispanic woman brought me into a small office where I met with the immigration officer. I couldn't tell if he was Filipino or Hispanic, but he certainly was not Caucasian. During the interview, he asked me how long I had lived in the States and inquired about what I did for a living. My response was the rehearsed answer Victor gave all of us, and I told him that I was a grape picker here for 10 years. The interview seemed totally staged to me because there was no way it should have been that quick and easy, especially based on my past experience with the "law," or more specifically with the U.S. Immigration officers in the Philippines. Without a doubt, they have a way of asking questions, and "easy and breezy" doesn't come to mind while they interrogated illegal aliens, ever! I was given an appointment to come back for a second interview, but it would not be for several months.

I was the last one to get back in the car this time, and Victor, much to my surprise, was actually smiling. "All done?" he inquired. "Yep," I responded, without any hint of being nervous. Then I picked up my green purse and looked at the zipper, which was now zipped all the way down the left side of the bag. *I knew it!* I thought, relieved. My intuition was right on target that Victor was just waiting for me to leave my bag so he could search it. Without a doubt, he was smiling because he didn't find anything as he initially suspected. *"Thank you, God, for saving and protecting me; now if you could just help me get the mini-recorder back, I would really appreciate it,"* I prayed in my head. We drove straight back to the couple's house, and as before, everyone needed to use the restroom. I decided to use the same tactic to reach the restroom upstairs.

Once I got inside the restroom, I turned on the water faucet and let it run to drown out any noise as I fumbled and searched quickly for the items I had left hidden in the cupboard. I was completely relieved when I found the rolled-up towel. Without hesitating, I put the mini-recorder and address book back in my bag. Then I flushed the toilet for full effect and shut the door on my way out. At this point, I doubt that Victor would have cared even if I wore my bag around my neck. He was relaxed and seemed appeased because he had the opportunity to rummage through my handbag earlier. We drove all the way back to Los Angeles very late that night. By the time I arrived at my grandma's house, I was thoroughly exhausted and fell straight into bed.

Chapter Five

Time to Hide

First thing the next morning, I got a call from Forman because we needed to discuss the case. As soon as I met with him, I gave him the mini-recorder. I had recorded some of the conversation from our driving time in the car, which included reminders and the specific instructions we were given at the house in Santa Maria. I wasn't sure how many tapes I went through or the extent of details recorded.

Forman praised me for the great job I had done, and he reassured me that all of the INS officers were very proud of me. In addition, he also told me that I was the first CI he had ever worked with who was actually smart and extremely brave.

Even though I appreciated his compliments and thanked him profusely, I empathically explained that there was no way I planned on going back to see Victor again. I explicitly detailed that it was simply a matter of time until Victor would realize what we were doing. Obviously he was very cunning and perceptive. Without hesitating, Forman informed me that there was no need to worry because the INS team had already decided not to send me back. Apparently, they were well aware that I just got lucky and realized that I came incredibly close to being caught by Victor. There wasn't much solace for me when Forman brought this up. Instead, it was a harsh and frightening reality for me to fully comprehend the ramifications of what I had done. Forman was pleased to inform me that they already had a load of evidence sufficient enough to put Victor behind bars. The INS still needed to do surveillance but wouldn't need me to meet with Victor ever again.

I was overcome with unbelievable relief until Forman stated, "At least not until you testify against him in court." I felt like I had just had a bucket of cold water thrown on my face. "Excuse me? What? What did you say? Are you telling me that I have to be in the same courtroom during his trial and face him again?" Forman gave me an obvious look of empathy and nodded his head yes saying, "This is part of the process, Corinna." This was startling new information for me. As far as I was concerned, we never discussed this, and in my world, it wasn't part of our deal. After the initial shock wore off a bit, I asked Forman if he merely forgot to mention this or if it was one of those "on a need-to-know basis" types of issues. Of course, I was well aware it was the latter, and at this point, I didn't really have any choice. Forman patiently reminded me, "You need to understand that you are the STAR WITNESS. Unfortunately, without your testimony, there would be no case. All the evidence we have collected, the pictures, conversations recorded, and even the paperwork would not mean anything or carry any credibility without you. You are a crucial part of this process with Victor and are in it for the long haul, so to speak." Then Forman explained in no uncertain terms that the only way I would be released from this process would be if Victor chose to plead guilty. No doubt, that is exactly what I would be hoping for.

After I regained my composure, I managed to ask, "So what do we do now?" "We simply wait," Forman answered matter-of-factly. Apparently, I was free now to take time off and to tour California. Forman encouraged me to spend some time with my family. Evidently, he and the INS team would call me when they needed me for anything. Forman also promised to keep me abreast of what was happening on a daily basis. This was encouraging to me because I know he was a man of his word who would do what he promised.

Before we parted, I inquired about when Maryl was supposed to come to the States. He patiently explained that I would put Maryl's life in danger if she lived with me during this time; without a doubt, it would be much safer for her to come to the United States after the trial was completed. I really had no idea how long that would be, but the last thing I wanted was to put my only daughter in danger. My heart was so heavy it actually hurt physically, but I managed to say "All right." After I arrived at Grandma Annie's house that night, I began to cry. I had absolutely no idea how long the trial would be, and even though I am not Sherlock Holmes, I definitely knew it would be a drawn-out process.

When I called Maryl that night, Stella picked up the phone. We didn't discuss anything that had to do with what I was doing because I couldn't tell anyone. It was all entirely "classified information." Obviously, those were words I never thought I would use, but now they had become a substantial part of my life. Stella told me stories about my precious daughter and related how much her mom and dad just loved Maryl to pieces. She also spoke about how Maryl took a nap with her dad in the recliner in the afternoons and described how her mom took Maryl to get groceries and shopping at the mall. Almost every day they went shopping together and then ate at a restaurant.

Each evening Maryl would curl up and sleep with Stella in her bedroom. In spite of her work during the weekdays, she would spend time with Maryl during her weekends off. Throughout the entire time she was telling me these stories, I kept crying on the other end of the line. I was careful to hide this and definitely didn't want Stella to know how painful the separation really was for me. Understandably, I was acutely jealous and upset that I was not the one spending time with Maryl and able to do all these things. It also really concerned me that Maryl was having so much fun; I was apprehensive that she would forget about me and eventually love the Santos family more than her own mother. After all, Maryl was only 3 years old, and at that age, children tend to forget very quickly. Truthfully, all the anxiety and stress created a very sick feeling in the pit of my stomach. It was almost unbearable.

Then Stella asked me, "Do you want to talk to her now?" Without any hesitation, I enthusiastically responded, "Oh yes, please, thank you." Maryl got on the phone, and I said, "Hi, baby, how are you?" It was very difficult, but I tried to sound jovial and upbeat while I was on the phone with her, despite my heart aching with loneliness. Her innocent voice simply responded, "Fine." Maryl's voice sounded somewhat bored, and it was evident that she was tired. I asked her what she was doing, and she just said, "Nothing." Little did she realize that I longed to hear her voice. Determined not to give up, I asked her if she missed me, and she simply said, "Yeah"; then she politely said, "Okay, bye Mommy." Despite my best efforts to keep her on the phone, continue to hear her sweet voice, and tell her how much I loved and missed her, she gave the phone back to Stella after what felt like only a few seconds. Stella apologized to me profusely and tried to assure me it was just the timing that evening. Stella explained to me that Maryl was busy playing with Stella's dad when I called and didn't really want to be interrupted while they had so much fun. "I could have done without that" was the first thing that came to my mind. My disappointment was evident, but I somehow muttered, "Okay." Before I hung up, I thanked Stella again for loving Maryl and taking such wonderful care of her. Finally, I asked her to thank her parents for me and let them know how much I appreciated their kindness and love.

When I got off the phone, I was devastated. My heart ached, and I couldn't breathe from crying so hard. For the first time in my life, I felt utterly helpless and was overcome with heartbreak. I was overwhelmed with grief. I didn't know where to turn my head and couldn't even find a position to be in to ease my pain and devastating anxiety. It seemed as if there was nothing I could possibly do. My thoughts were desperate: *What if, after all of this, I end up losing the love of my life, my only child?* This thought repeatedly tormented me for a while before I finally managed to fall asleep.

The next few weeks were very desolate and depressing. Even so, the work that I was doing for the INS started to feel more fulfilling despite the continual danger it presented. At least I didn't have to continually watch the time, and I found my adrenalin was always pumping. The exhilaration certainly gave me some kind of a high sensation.

I hadn't seen or spoken to my dad and his wife since the night he kicked me out of his house. And I was not allowed to get a job yet; that wouldn't be an option until the Mabuhay case was closed. I called Maryl often, but the conversations were always predictable and heart wrenching for me. She barely spoke, and I felt like she was pulling further away from me. Amidst the emotional intensity and weariness, I was starting to lose the desire to live in the United States. I was losing my aspiration and focus on why I had to fight to get to the States in the first place until I got a phone call that would change my circumstances.

When I picked up the phone, I heard Forman's voice. He asked if I was available to meet with him and talk. Of course, he immediately reminded me that we couldn't talk about this confidential information over the phone. From our brief preliminary conversation, I became both excited and anxious at the same time. Although I didn't know what had happened, I could tell there was a new development on the Mabuhay case. I met Forman at a coffee shop. I spoke first, before I even sat down, and I began asking him what was going on. He told me, "We have to move you as soon as possible." Of course, my response was, "Why?" Much to my surprise, Forman retorted, "Because we are ready to make an arrest. We will have to move simultaneously because of the 16-hour time difference. The U.S. team will be in position at Victor's residence in the middle of the night, and the Philippine team will be at Manuel's office around 10:00 in the morning." "But why do I have to hide? Does Victor know it was me who set him up?" I inquired.

Forman assured me that Victor did not know right then, but as soon as he was interrogated, he would find out because they would have to show him everything they had against him. That would include all of the pictures, the surveillance videos, the files, and more important, the recorded conversation they had on him. Somehow, this information must have created a total panic for me because once I heard this, I started to feel my head throbbing; my ears felt like they were clogged with water; and all of a sudden, my chest hurt and I found it difficult to catch my breath. It truly felt like a full-blown asthma attack. During this time, my head started to swirl with several thoughts, and I pounded Forman with questions and emotionally charged words: "Where will I go? What about Maryl? When is she coming here? There is no way I am going anywhere or doing anything unless I see her. You promised me she would be here two weeks after I arrived, yet it has been a month and I haven't seen my daughter. I don't care if you have to deport me or if I never have to step foot in your country ever again! The only reason I agreed to do this was for my child, and if she is not here, I am going home! I don't care anymore!"

I honestly think Forman was completely taken aback with my reaction because he looked a bit shell-shocked. Up to this point I had been compliant. For the first time, I think he finally realized that I meant what I had been saying all along, that this really was all for my daughter's future. Forman had mentioned previously to me that I was the only CI they had worked with who was not intimidated by the officer or their authority. Well, so they thought. Actually, what they didn't know about me was that I had perfected, at a very young age, the art of not showing fear, humiliation, hurt, or pain. I had to. This hiding of emotions was my only means of surviving my dad's wrath.

Papa Stay …
❀

"If I see even just a teardrop on your face, I am going to beat you harder! So you better not cry!" I must have been only 4 or 5 years old the first time my dad laid down this steadfast rule: No crying allowed. I could never understand why he hated to see my sister and me cry. Each time I got beaten, I had to hold back the tears because he meant every word of what he said. My dad has this violent temper. He could be in a really good mood; then, in just a matter of a split second, he would yell so loud you would wish you had crawled under the bed and disappeared before he started his tirade.

One of the most memorable beatings I ever got was when I was in elementary school. I can't even remember what I did that day, but I recall that my mom was sitting across the room from the couch on which my dad and I were sitting. He was yelling at me relentlessly about something. I was standing in front of him trying to anticipate when he would hit me. He had a definite pattern. First, he would order me to sit or stand across from him; then he would stare at me up and down from the top of my head to the bottom of my toes, sizing me up. All the time, he would make sounds that represented intense disapproval. Sadly, this usually conveyed his extreme regret and unbelief about whatever I had said or done.

Then he would ask questions like, "What prompted you to do that anyway?" I remember not ever knowing what to answer because it really didn't matter what I said anyway. When he would reach this point, there was definitely no turning back. I would always get beaten, and it never mattered what I said. Throughout this ordeal, he would ask the same question over and over again: "Do you understand me?" At this point, I would usually squirm a little bit or tense up my body to prepare myself. I could never accurately tell when it would happen; usually by the third or fourth question his first blow would come and hit me with such intensity. He always called the shots, and there was no way to know either where he would strike me again or what side of my body would get hit.

My dad would usually try to hit me on my side. Nevertheless, on that particular day, he was so angry that he grabbed his leather slippers that were about two inches thick and started hitting me repeatedly. At one point, he literally hit me on the head with such force that blood began to squirt out. On this particular occasion, my mom even started crying and yelling at him, begging him to stop. It was so bad that she even fainted. At this point my dad stopped beating me and angrily screamed, "If anything happens to your mom, I am going to kill you." Believe it or not, when he said that, it didn't scare me at all. For some strange reason, what it did was give me some hope in my heart that my mom and dad would somehow mend their relationship. I clearly remember thinking to myself, My dad still loves my mom; if he didn't, why would he care if she fainted?

I am 53 years old now. Just recently, one of my friends told me her mom and dad were getting back together after being divorced for 15 years. Even at my age, there are times when I still wish that my mom and dad would be together too. I don't really understand why I never gave up on them, and in my heart I still long for them to be a couple—yes, even to this day. My sister used to laugh at me and thought I was too idealistic. In fact, she still does today. Once in a while she will tell me, "You're such a dreamer and too dramatic." In addition, she continues to tell me that I am way too sensitive.

My sister is only 11 months older than I am. She was born in June of 1962, and I was born in May of 1963. Our mom was only 16 years old when my sister was born, and our dad was 20. Without a doubt, this explained part of the reason why I ended up in the care of my Grandma Lola. The age gap between my sister and me was too close, and our parents were way too young; it was literally children raising children. When our mom and dad finally decided to go their separate ways, I was 8 years old and my sister was 9. There was no such thing as divorce in the Philippines. Therefore, married people simply separate and live apart on their own.

It must have been early in the evening when our dad asked my sister and me to come out of our bedroom to talk. We were definitely wondering what was going on because my dad really didn't sound angry or mad. In fact, he had a somber expression on his face that day. Dad asked us to come sit with him and our mom, who was already in the living room. As soon as my sister and I sat down, my dad matter-of-factly said, "Your mom and I are separating. I want you both to choose whom you would like to live with." And that was that. There was no explanation or further conversation.

I don't know what my sister thought, but I was completely taken by surprise. Up to that point in time, I didn't even know that married people ever separated. Every married couple in our family that I was exposed to, both on my dad's side of the family and my mom's, was together. So the word "separation" was foreign and totally new to me.

As a young child, I was utterly confused. Sure, I was aware that my mom and dad fought all the time. Their fighting was so intense that quite often my sister and I would either hide under our bed or conceal our squeezed bodies in the corner of our bed, hiding. For the duration of their powerful fights, we would even cover our ears to drown out their yelling.

Despite the intensity of their fights, however, somehow they always managed to make up. It was surprising that even though they would get very violent sometimes, somehow they would always talk and appear all right the next day. Now here we sat as my dad calmly told us that, after all that, they were separating! My first inclination was to call my Grandma Lola and have her fix it. She lived three houses down on our street. My sister and I would usually pound on her door, even as early as three o'clock in the morning, whenever our mom and dad fiercely fought. She would come and set our parents straight. After all, they were scared of her. However, there was such a blatant finality in my dad's tone, I was consciously aware this was no longer an option.

Everything felt surreal, and I couldn't believe this was happening to us. It had only been three years since my mom stopped dropping me off and picking me up at my Grandma Lola's house, and I was just starting to enjoy living with my whole family. My mom and dad both had secure jobs. My parents were making good money, we had a nice car, and we ate well and wore good clothes. We were going to one of the most expensive private schools and didn't lack for anything. Even though my parents fought all the time, I sincerely felt this was much better than being without them living together. My thoughts were interrupted when I heard my sister say, "I am going with you, Papa." He seemed relieved and pleased with her response.

Then he turned to me and said, "Okay, what about you, Corinna?" I looked at my mom; she was sitting quietly. I assumed she was very sad about my sister's announcement. I began to think about what would happen to her if my sister and I both went with our dad. Dad had much more money than she did. If she lost both of her children, how would she ever be able to deal with the overwhelming loneliness?

Without any hesitation, I responded, "I am going with Mama." My dad didn't say much, but he quickly got up and told my sister he would come back to get her. He quietly left the room, got dressed, packed his suitcase, and then loaded his car. I was watching him load his belongings through the screen of our front door. Dad climbed into his car and shut the door; then he put his arms around the steering wheel and started to cry uncontrollably. When he was able to regain his composure, he put the car in reverse and slowly backed out of our driveway. Everything within me wanted to run after my dad and beg him not to leave, but before I could even move, he was gone.

Just like that, my whole life changed right before my very eyes. It took awhile before my dad came back to pick up my sister. I don't know exactly why. Luckily, I wasn't nearly as lonely as I thought I was going to be because with my dad gone, we actually experienced a little bit of peace at the house. For the first time, there was no yelling or fighting happening in our home. My sister and I were able to continue to go to our private school. I was in third grade at the time, and she was in fourth grade. We only saw our dad once a week. He would come see us every Friday at our school. Although I sincerely looked forward to seeing him, I noticed my dad wasn't nearly as warm with me as he was with my sister.

Whenever he showed up at our school, he would always ask us how things were at home and inquire as to whether we were okay. I also noticed that he never really asked about our mom, at least not that I was aware of. My dad was pretty popular at our school because he was so very personable with everyone there. They all liked him a lot and thought he was good-looking. I also felt this way about my dad. I always thought my dad was the most handsome of all his siblings in his younger days. He dressed exceptionally well and was always impeccably groomed. Whenever he came to our school, he wouldn't leave until he went to our cafeteria. He would take my sister and me with him and say to the manager who worked there, "These are my children. If for some reason they run out of money before the end of the week, please give them anything they want. I am here every Friday, and I will settle with you when I return."

As a result, the manager was always more than willing to open a tab for us. This was especially crucial for me because I ate so much. My sister and I would take a lunch packed from home every day, and I always ate my food and drank two bottles of "Chocó bim" (this was like Nestlé chocolate milk) before our actual lunch break began. Then when lunchtime came around, I would go to the cafeteria and tell the manager, "I want the fried chicken lunch today, please." I used to allow my schoolmates, even some who were not my friends, to get what they wanted in the cafeteria. "Don't worry about it," I would tell them, and I was always incredibly generous.

I can still remember how shocked my dad was the first time he walked over to the cafeteria to settle our bill. The manager said he owed 500 pesos. This was in the 1970s and was a lot of money. My dad couldn't believe the bill, and he kept saying, "What could you have possibly eaten, and how much did you eat?" Fortunately, I didn't get spanked, and he didn't even yell at me. I believe that for the most part my dad was just in utter disbelief. Not surprisingly, after that day, he put a limit on our account, that it would no longer exceed 200 pesos. In reality, this wasn't bad at all considering we already brought our lunches from home every day.

Truthfully, I was kind of a difficult child. I would get angry very easily, and none of my teachers particularly liked me. You could often find me in the principal's office. Without a doubt, I was quite the outcast. In fact, my third-grade teacher even threatened to fail the other students if they spoke to me, so I was completely alone during that school year. I acted like I didn't care, and I didn't even try to get anyone to talk to me. Despite all this, I was never afraid of my teachers or intimidated by them.

One of my main tasks was to be my sister's defender. No one messed with her except for Rodolfo, and he was the school principal's grandson. He was also one of my sister's classmates. One day, I found my sister sitting on a bench crying her eyes out. It took awhile, and I had to force her to tell me what was bothering her. She eventually told me, "Rodolfo lifted up my skirt in front of the class." I walked away from her without saying anything and immediately went to the playground searching for Rodolfo. When I finally found him, I picked up a dustpan made of tin and smacked him in the face with it. The force of the hit cut him on the cheek, which instantly started to bleed. As soon as he realized he was bleeding, Rodolfo pushed and shoved me so hard that I sat on a barbwire, which deeply cut my left thigh. The cut was so bad that I thought I was going to need stitches. However, even that incident didn't make me cry, not a tear! I had perfected my emotional hiding.

Agent Jimenez found a place for me to hide. He placed me at the Mission Hills hotel in Simi Valley, California. Although it wasn't a five-star hotel, it wasn't really that bad either. This place was located on an incredibly busy street. It was a sparse, brown building that had a spiral staircase and an elevator to get to my room, which was on the second floor. The lobby was modest but clean. Most of the clientele who came in and out of the place were businessmen. Directly across the street were several office buildings. Jimenez took care of the paperwork for me at the front desk. He told me I could go to my room to check it out, so I happily did. My room had two queen-sized beds, a table with two chairs, a television set, and a tiny refrigerator. Everything about it was completely brown. All the bedding and the furniture were the same dingy color. My favorite thing was the balcony that overlooked the Valley. *This would definitely help ease a bit of the hotel feeling of being stuck,* I thought.

I also took the opportunity to look for the exits, just in case Victor ever discovered where I was staying. There was an exit door that was only two rooms down on the left side of the hallway. While I was standing on the balcony, I checked to see if I could, if necessary, jump from the balcony down to the streets. It appeared to be a possibility, but Victor could also come after me by jumping from the ground onto my balcony. However, I decided not to worry about that at this point. Instead, I determined that I would just double lock the door at all times.

After about 30 minutes, Jimenez came up to my room and let me know that the hotel paperwork was completed and that the bill had already been taken care of so I didn't need to worry. He then reiterated that it was critically important for me not to tell anyone, including my family, where I was staying. In fact, I was not even allowed to call them or make any sort of contact because this would endanger them as well. Next he asked me to double-check all the telephone numbers I had in case I had to make an emergency call. Before he left, he looked at me and said, "Okay, I have to go now. Stay safe, and we will keep in touch," before he walked out and shut the door behind him. Suddenly, I stood in my room all alone and felt cut off from everyone. I didn't really have very much to unpack, so it only took me a short time to put all my clothes away. I opened the blinds and drapes to allow for additional light in the room. Then I sat down at the table facing the streets and watched the cars go by. With a heavy heart, I realized that I didn't even get to say goodbye to Grandma Annie.

Chapter Six

Maryl Arrives

The next two days passed quietly and without incident. Jimenez would call randomly to check in with me and to ask how I was doing. His personality was very different from Forman's. Unquestionably, Jimenez came across as distant and cold. In reality he wasn't, but this was his professional personality. I made sure to get some exercise each day by walking all around the area and to help avoid sinking into any further depression. My meals consisted solely of take-out food. Somehow I didn't really care about this because I honestly didn't have an appetite anyway. Because I received a per diem from the INS, I didn't have to use any of the money I brought with me, and they gladly took care of my expenses.

By the third day of waiting, I got a call from Forman. He called to let me know he was going to stop by to discuss the case with me. Forman was pleased to inform me that Victor had been taken into custody earlier that morning. Once again, he reminded me about the distinct possibility of having to testify against Victor in the event he didn't plead guilty. This reminder couldn't have come at a better time because it gave me the opportunity to play my "star witness" card. In a very stern and serious manner, I asked him directly when I would be seeing my daughter again. Not surprisingly, his response was, "As soon as this is over." Yet I refused to accept that response anymore. So I clearly told him I was not willing to wait any longer because I felt my daughter was slowly drifting away from me. Then I demanded with a calm tone, "It's Thursday today. If Maryl is not here by Monday, I am going back to the Philippines." By that very evening, Forman informed me that Maryl would be arriving on Saturday with my best friend, Stella. For the first time since I had arrived in the States, I was completely overjoyed! I was so excited that I barely slept that night or for the next few nights until Saturday came. At last, the important moment finally arrived, and at 6:00 p.m., Forman drove me to LAX to pick up Maryl and Stella.

Maryl and Stella would be waiting for me at the INS office. Because I was a paroled immigrant, Maryl would have to get the same paperwork and follow with the agreement I had already made. Her papers read: "To enter the United States as an alien paroled pursuant to Section 212(d)(5)(A) of the Immigration and Nationality Act." Remarks: PAROLED AUTHORIZED PURSUANT TO TELECON WITH CENTRAL OFFICE, WASHINGTON D.C.

My friend Stella was given a six-month tourist visa, as a courtesy from INS, which I thought was a very nice gesture. Forman and I drove to the airport in total silence. I couldn't even talk because I was far too concerned about Maryl's reaction and how things were going to be for us. I was still worried that she would have forgotten me and afraid she would not want to stay with me anymore. *What was I going to do if she asked Stella to take her back home?* I wondered. I could hardly sit still and wait while Forman parked the INS car. It took all my self-control to not just hop out of the car and start running. Probably the only thing that kept me from doing so was the fact that I didn't know where we were going and I needed Forman to lead me the private way into the INS office that was located at LAX. As soon as we stepped out of the car in what seemed like a labyrinth, I started to press Forman, "Where is she?" My anticipation was overwhelming. Forman calmly motioned for me to keep walking, and he gestured to the room in front of us located on the right.

As soon as I walked in, I immediately spotted her! There was my Maryl. I couldn't believe how much she had already grown since our last time together. She was wearing a beautiful pink dress with a pink headband, pink socks, and black patent-leather shoes. She looked like a princess and was sitting slightly slumped over on a chair (obviously tired from her long trip) with her favorite doll, Cricket, on her lap. "Maryl anak!" I exclaimed. This meant "my daughter" in my native language. She looked up at me and said, "Mommy!" which was sweet music to my ears. I burst into tears as I picked her up and held her tightly in my arms. I couldn't stop kissing her repeatedly. I told her, over and over, how much I had missed her and how happy I was that she was finally with me; I vowed never to be separated from her again. Forman was noticeably very happy for me; because he had three children whom he loved very much, he understood my overwhelming joy. I finally managed to give Stella a big hug but wouldn't put Maryl down; I then thanked her for all she had done for us. On our drive away from the airport, we stopped at Denny's to grab a bite to eat before proceeding to our hotel. That night, I had the best sleep ever. Just having my daughter sleep beside me with my arms wrapped around her made me forget about all that I had recently been through. I thank God for that momentous day.

When I woke up the next morning, I cuddled with Maryl for a bit before moving. I asked her what she wanted to do that day. Because I had not really explored the area where we were, Stella decided we should do some shopping. She suggested we go purchase a microwave for our hotel room so we would be able to heat up food and have the freedom to eat meals other than fast food. We studied the bus routes schedule until we were more familiar with locations and times. All of us were dressed in thick jackets even though it was only November. We were cold. When we all started to descend the staircase of our hotel, I literally felt like I was walking on air. All of a sudden, for the first time, I was aware of my surroundings and realized how gorgeous the flowers were, how the streets were so clean, and how beautiful the mountains were. In fact, I was actually singing, and my joy was overflowing.

Our first stop was at a store that carried all sorts of electronic stuff. I bought a small microwave, a JVC radio cassette player, and an electric typewriter. I thought it was important that my speed in typing didn't diminish. Before I had left the Philippines, I typed 80 words per minute, and I knew it was extremely important to maintain that speed in order to obtain a future job.

Luckily, Stella wasn't as geographically challenged as I was, so we were able to find the places we planned to visit. We also visited her aunt, and it was wonderful to be able to eat a home-cooked meal. Her aunt had no idea about what was going on with any of us; of course, we couldn't tell her either. During this lovely time, we even went to San Francisco. I can still remember looking at the famous bridge there, and I did not understand why it was called the Golden Gate Bridge. The color of the bridge didn't look like gold to me at all, and I distinctly remember thinking it was a definite rusty color. Finally someone from the Bay Area explained to me that when the sun hits the bridge, it appears to look like gold.

One day, Forman stopped by our hotel and took all of us out to dinner. During our meal, he gave me the great news that I wouldn't need to testify against Victor. Apparently he was intelligent enough to realize they had overwhelming evidence against him. Victor was found guilty on 15 counts, yet he pled guilty on only five counts and was given a mere five years in prison with the possibility of parole for good behavior. "Seriously, good behavior?" I said, thinking that was ironic. Of course, the Mabuhay case brought in a lot of cash because everything they seized from Victor now was the property of INS. There were Rolex watches, a brand-new Mercedes-Benz, thousands of dollars in cash, and additional money stashed in a bank under Victor's name. Forman further explained that I could finally come out of hiding. I could now start to live my life, and even more important, I was free to get a job! I was so happy I could barely grasp what he told me.

In addition, he informed me he was going to return to the Philippines where he was originally stationed. As soon as I realized Forman was actually leaving, I couldn't help but feel a sense of loneliness and fear. Truly, Forman was the one person in the United States I completely trusted, and he had proven himself to be trustworthy. God was so good to me and had sent Forman my way to protect and take care of me during this difficult time. Now he was leaving; whom would I run to when I encountered problems? At the moment it was as if Forman read my mind, because he reassured me by saying, "Jimenez will take it from here. He will see to it that you and Maryl are safe and protected at all times. He is a good man, and you can trust him." Forman also reminded me that until I received the final approval of my dad's petition for me as the daughter of a U.S. citizen, which was approximately five years away, I was legally bound to the contract I had signed with the INS. Therefore, I had to continue working for U.S. Immigration as an undercover or confidential informant whenever they needed me. Unfortunately, I didn't have the luxury of saying no. I was also instructed never to give my address or telephone number to anyone other than for employment purposes.

After he got done explaining everything to me, Forman had to leave. Saying goodbye to Forman was bittersweet. He did mention that he was working on getting transferred back to the United States. I just hoped that he would come back soon because I was still afraid of Jimenez. Stella was contemplating staying, but she soon ended up flying back home instead. Watching her leave was extremely painful for me. I loved her dearly, and I wanted her to stay with us in the States. I thought it would be wonderful for the three of us to start our lives together. However, in the end Stella decided it would be better to go back to the Philippines.

For the first time in our lives, Maryl and I were totally alone. This time, however, I didn't mind it too much because we were together. Once again, I was very excited about the prospect that we could start our life over in the United States. Now I would be able to raise my daughter in a country that didn't condemn unwed mothers who made foolish choices. My daughter would have the opportunity to grow up in an environment that allowed people the freedom to thrive despite their social status. I was thankful that Maryl would be raised in an atmosphere that would call her by her real name and not label her a "bastard."

Mary Magdalene
🌺

The thought of going back home seemed unfathomable to me now. I remember the church in the Philippines we went to every Sunday. It was a small Catholic church that was specifically built for the subdivision where we lived. Maryl and I regularly attended the 6:00 p.m. service. Usually, there were at least 25–30 people at the service. Everyone knew each other but not intimately. People knew where each other lived and were aware of whom they lived with. They also knew about each member's source of livelihood or personal career. It truthfully wouldn't be surprising to me if they each knew how much money everyone else made. All this information was acquired by word of mouth and then passed from one person to another. I can vividly remember one of the services Maryl and I attended on Good Friday. The reading that service was about Mary Magdalene. While the priest taught about what type of a woman she was according to the Bible, he looked straight at me throughout the service, and so did the eyes of every person who was part of the congregation on that evening. I felt like there was an intense heat right above my head that poured down upon me like a huge spotlight. It felt like everyone was staring at me, referring to me like "ta-da" I was the modern-day Mary Magdalene.

My first impulse was to stand up and run out of the church as quickly as humanly possible and never come back. Because I was stuck sitting in the middle of the pew totally surrounded by people, I simply sat there pretending I didn't understand that the priest was referring to me and using this as an example for the congregation. Unfortunately, that was not a smart move on my part because it only made the priest glare at me even more intensely. Surprisingly, the strange thing about this incident was that despite the shame and hurt inflicted on me, I continued to go back every Sunday evening. I guess I thought of it as a penance for my wayward ways, thinking, I am, after all, a single mother with a child born out of wedlock.

Obviously I believed that I was supposed to suffer and pay the price because I had committed a great sin. I had been raised in a very religious family. I remember my Grandma Lola had her own interpretation of Matthew 19:24: "Again I say to you, it is easier for a camel to go through the eye of a needle, than for a rich man to enter the kingdom of God." Grandma Lola told us this Scripture meant that God doesn't like rich people. In addition, she said the more you suffer the better because God would love you even more from your sharing in His suffering on the cross. I lived with all sorts of guilt.

Even when I was raped at 13 years old, I somehow thought that was my fault. I must have done something to cause this man to rape me, I told myself repeatedly until I had convinced myself that it was my fault and something that I deserved. Sadly, I never even told anyone what happened to me after I was raped and, as a result, carried that shame and guilt by myself.

I used to pray the rosary once a week or during Lent season until I got pregnant; then I prayed it daily. My petition determined how often I would pray. For a whole year, before my trip to the United States, I prayed the rosary at least seven times a day. I also took a trip to a very popular church in Baclaran, Manila. There were people there from all walks of life. They came from various towns, provinces, and cities to pay their homage and to pray the novena to the Virgin Mary, who was lovingly referred to as the "Mother of Perpetual Help." The novena (which was a small booklet filled with prayers, incantations, and chanting recitations) was held every Wednesday, and the service went on all day, every hour, by the hour. If I am not mistaken, the first service starts at six in the morning. The priests usually held a mass first and then proceeded to the novena part of the service. I would guess about 1,000 to 1,500 people attended the Wednesday novenas. This church was more like a cathedral because it was huge and very beautiful.

From the gate entrance to the church door, you had to walk about half a mile. Entering the gates, you were immediately greeted by vendors who sold various items such as different kinds of charms that were supposed to protect a person from all sorts of voodoo and bad luck. They also had a "Santo Nino," which literally means "a *small baby Jesus"; strings of sampaguita, which was the Philippines national flower for its sweet aroma and beauty; and different food! There were all kinds of food, from "chitcheria" (snacks) to barbecued pork, beef, chicken feet, animal blood, porridge, and cotton candy. All kinds of drinks were also sold—soda, "sago at gulaman," which was jello in very sweet syrup, and all sorts of juices. If you could make a juice out of a turnip, they would sell it there.*

Most people like me who attended regularly had perfected a special way to maneuver away from all these vendors. It was necessary to be very good at evading most of them because the vendors who sold the charms were very slick and professional. They would march right straight up into your face, with no fear of or regard for your personal space. Then they would try to pin one of their charms on your shirt or dress with the possibility of digging into or taking a tiny bite of your skin, and this was usually on your chest. Talk about violating one's space.

Once you made it past all that commotion, at the door of the church there was a small room that had several sculptures of saints, like St. Jude, Joseph, Michael, and numerous others. In the middle of this room was a marble stand filled with holy water. Everyone who entered would have to dip a finger or two into the water and make the sign of the cross while reciting out loud, "In the name of the Father, the Son, and the Holy Spirit." Even though almost everyone would pray to the saints while they waited for the novena to start, I did not.

When I arrived, the first thing I would do was drop to my knees right at the entrance and then take out my rosary beads. I walked on my knees while reciting the 15 mysteries of the rosary. The distance from the entrance door to the main altar was about 10 yards, give or take. I religiously performed this ritual every Wednesday. This was especially true when I got pregnant. My sins felt like they were so great, and it was the only way I knew how to absolve myself. In spite of all this, a priest once told me that there was no absolution for the way I was leading my life. This was disappointing for me to hear, but there was something deep inside of me that strongly believed God was merciful to even me, so I continued with these rituals despite that priest's disheartening words. As a matter of fact, it was at that particular place when I prayed for a girl after I found out that I was pregnant. I was so devoted I prayed, "Virgin Mary, if you will let me have a girl, I will name her after you." Hence, my daughter's name is Mary Louise, but I simply called her Maryl for short.

Chapter Seven

Life in the United States

I started calling my relatives to let them know that Maryl and I were beginning to search for a place to live. Even though my Grandma Annie was an obvious option, I decided that I would prefer not to pursue this option because I wanted for Maryl and me to have our own privacy. In addition, my dad went to her house quite often, and I was afraid it would upset him if we lived with her. One of my first cousins offered us an empty bedroom in her home for only $300. This included the utilities, and I would share the expense of food. She had two wonderful boys. One was Maryl's age, and the other son was just two years older. She was also very kind and helped me get a job at the company she worked for. My job wasn't glamorous at all, and I was hired as a gofer. As a matter of fact, initially they didn't want to hire me because they told me I was overqualified for the job. I assured them that I really needed this job and that it didn't matter to me. In fact, I didn't care about this at all; to me it was simply a job that I needed. I was confident enough to know that I would be able to work my way up to another position. Besides, it was not in me to complain; after all, a job is a job!

My cousin readily sold me her stick shift red Nissan Sentra. It already had 16,000 miles on it; there was no air-conditioning. It was either a year old or less, and it was a good car for me. I assumed the loan from her, and Maryl and I moved in with her right away, totally thrilled to move out of the motel. Maryl was excited to be with her second cousins, and I was happy to feel like we finally had some sort of normalcy in our lives. Initially, we didn't have our own bed, so my cousin let us use one of her twin bed mattresses, which we set in the middle of the floor. Our bedroom was quite small with no furniture except for a small bookshelf. I placed my JVC stereo on that as well as some books that I bought to read. My cousin suggested Maryl go to the same babysitter with her two sons. Although I surely struggled with the thought, there was no other option at the time. I had no choice but to start working.

My cousin instructed me to take her two boys and Maryl to the sitter first thing in the morning and then pick them all up in the afternoon, which I did reluctantly. The first day I had to drop off the children at the babysitter's house, I was extremely concerned because I didn't know anything about these people. The only consolation I had was that the boys were already there. I knew that if their mom said the sitter was okay, she must be all right. Why else would she leave her two boys there? She was a great mother to them. When I said goodbye to them, the boys were used to it and didn't seem to care. However, Maryl looked up at me, with her eyes filled with tears, and asked me, "Where are you going, Mommy?" It broke my heart, but I tried not to cry as I took the time to explain to her that she didn't have her nanny or Stella to care for her anymore. I further explained that I had to work now for a living, "so I need for you to behave yourself and listen to the babysitter, okay?" Even though she seemed like she wanted to cry, she sweetly said, "Okay, Mommy." Somehow she held it together, for my sake.

My Sweet Maryl
❀

Maryl has always been a fantastic child. She was born in December of 1984, after three difficult days of labor. My doctor was concerned that I was going to have a C-section, but I was grateful it was a normal birth even though I was induced. I vividly remember passing out right after her birth. When I woke up it was almost noon. I was still in severe pain, but it was bearable. I am almost certain that being 21 years old made it easier to recover quickly.

I gathered up all my leftover strength to put on my bathrobe and walk over to the nursery to see my new baby daughter. What overwhelming bliss to view Maryl in the nursery room with the rest of the babies. She wasn't crying at all, just sleeping amidst all the noise around her. I wondered if babies got worn out from the birthing process. As I stood there staring at her, I couldn't believe this tiny human being had actually been inside me, and I found myself overcome with emotions.

It wasn't too long before I had to go back to my room because I got very dizzy. About two hours later, the nurse carried in this perfect swaddle and asked me to breastfeed Maryl. I was incredibly careful when the nurse handed her to me; I didn't want to hurt her. She was only 6 pounds, 12 ounces. Like every new mom, I was concerned that I would accidentally break a bone or hurt her in some way. The moment she was in my arms, I felt an overwhelming delight well up inside of me. And I distinctly remember making a vow to her on that particular day, "You will never, ever have to go through what I have been through, ever."

The first six months of Maryl's life were very difficult and frightening for me, because I wasn't sure that I knew what I was supposed to be doing. Unfortunately, she was a colicky infant. Maryl would sleep peacefully all day but then would cry from 9:00 p.m. to 6:00 a.m. Of course, I totally blamed myself for this because during my pregnancy I ate too much chocolate and drank a lot of soda. My diet was extremely poor, but I don't recall my OB-GYN telling me I wasn't supposed to eat huge bars of Hershey's dark chocolate or drink a liter of soda every day. I did this in addition to eating four full meals each day. At the beginning of my first trimester, I weighed 109 pounds, but by the time I was ready to give birth, I weighed 165 pounds. I was so big that I would cry when I saw myself in the mirror because my reflection didn't even look anything like I normally did. Then it took me a year to get back to my original weight.

As far as I was concerned, everything seemed completely normal except for the occasional incidents when Maryl choked during her breastfeeding. Whenever this happened, I would immediately stop her feeding, turn her around slowly, and then give her a very light pat on the back. Because this happened quite frequently, I just assumed it was normal. Whenever I did mention this to her pediatrician, he explained to me that I needed to elevate Maryl's head whenever I would breastfeed her. He told me she choked because she ate too fast and therefore would suck air in the process. He assured me that this was "nothing to worry about." He was one of the best pediatricians at Makati Medical Center in the Philippines at that time.

When we went home that day I was relieved. The next few days Maryl was breastfeeding well, and I was doing everything the doctor recommended. For a while there, all seemed to be working according to plan. In fact, she even gained two pounds during this season. Shortly after, however, one night while I was breastfeeding Maryl, she started to choke again. Without hesitation, I proceeded to do my usual routine, except this time Maryl completely stopped breathing and turned blue! I became frantic and started to panic as I kept yelling, "Maryl, Maryl! Oh my God, please help me! What am I supposed to do? God, please, NO! Please help me!" I laid her down on the bed and started to give her mouth-to-mouth resuscitation. She was so tiny and frail that I was afraid I wasn't going to do it correctly and would end up killing her by accident, but I did it anyway. It must have worked because it wasn't long before she started to breathe again, and then her natural color came back. I hugged her ever so tightly and started to rock her back and forth while sobbing and thanking God continually for giving her precious life back to me.

When Maryl fell back to sleep, I dropped down on my knees. As I held my rosary beads, I prayed the rosary of all 15 mysteries of the cross. When I got down to the last bead, which was the "Hail Holy Queen" recitation, I promised God that I would pray the rosary seven times per day until He healed Maryl. I also asked forgiveness for my sins and promised God that I would mend my ways. Still, I pleaded with God, "Just don't take her away from me, please." While I begged, I honestly thought God was punishing me for bringing a child into the world outside of marriage. After that night, my life was changed forever. I couldn't really sleep anymore. From that day forward, I would constantly wake up during the night to check and see if my daughter was breathing.

The only other time I had to check for someone's breathing was when I was 9 years old. Too often, I would find my mom passed out on the floor. Whenever this would happen I tended to think she was dead, so I would get down on the floor and listen to her breathe to make sure she was still alive. At 9 years old I didn't know she just had one too many drinks.

Even when Maryl was asleep during the day, I would lay my head on her chest to make sure she was still breathing. I never left her side for anything unless I had to go to the bathroom. This was the only time her nanny would take her for me. Otherwise, Maryl was always with me, almost 24/7, and I didn't trust anyone else to care for her at all. By the time Maryl turned a year old, she was completely free of the "choking" syndrome. Later I found out it wasn't really a syndrome. Maryl's lungs were not fully developed when she was born. Actually, the doctors should not have allowed her to go home with me, and she should have been in an incubator until her lungs were developed. Naturally, I blamed myself for her physical challenges too because I was an avid smoker before I became pregnant. Granted, I completely stopped smoking when I realized that I was pregnant. However, I don't know if that made much of a difference or if I stopped soon enough to not impact her development.

Maryl was potty-trained by 12 months old, and she also transitioned from a bottle to drinking her milk from a plastic baby cup by this time. When she was a baby and tried to suck her thumb, I put a little bitter mixture on it. Fortunately, that is all it took for her to never want to pursue sucking her thumb again. She ate with her nanny and me at the table for both lunch and dinner sitting in her own high chair and contentedly eating her baby food. My sweet child was such a good little girl; I don't recall her ever giving me any problem. I never thought I could love anyone as much as I loved and adored her. From dawn till dusk, we spent our days together, and they were filled with fun and laughter. She was my life! We would do various things:

We went shopping, I took her to the zoo, we spent time at the park, I read her books each day, and we always played together. When she was 3 years old, we played dress-up together. I would put some makeup on her, and she would wear her beautiful dresses. Usually, I let her borrow my heels and big dangle earrings, and then we took some pictures. Maryl was always "picture ready." She also danced and sang on command, never too shy to perform. She spoke like a grown-up person and had a vocabulary well advanced for her age. She was able to carry on a conversation and could easily order her own meal. Maryl was a happy child and was easy to raise.

Now, for the first time in her life, Maryl would be left with a woman she had never even met before. This woman was supposed to care for her all day while I was at work. After I kissed Maryl goodbye, I quickly turned away because I didn't want her to see me crying. That day I asked God to protect her and her cousins. It didn't take long to quickly forget how sad I was when I realized I was on my way to my brand-new job. I would be working on Colorado Blvd., in Southern California. Before I put my red Nissan Sentra into gear, I reviewed the directions to work that my cousin had written for me on a piece of paper. Her directions instructed me to take the 5 freeway south and exit Colorado Blvd. I got on the 134 west freeway from Glendale and then continued driving on the 5 freeway.

Everything was strange and was all so new to me. Driving on the freeway here in the United States doesn't even come close to driving in the Philippines. The lanes back home were more like a decoration than necessity. People drove crazy over there, including myself. Anyone could change lanes at any time from the left or the right lane. In addition, we could go any speed we wanted. It was all about defensive driving. While I drove on the freeway, I kept examining my surroundings and looking at all the green boards with the white writing on them. I remembered my cousin saying that I needed to read those signs in order to not miss my off-ramp. I was very stressed out trying to read everything and figure out where I was headed, while I tried to adjust to the flow of traffic.

After driving for a bit, I started to wonder if I was going in the right direction. All of a sudden, I realized I had been driving for about an hour, and I still hadn't seen the Colorado Blvd. exit. I kept driving anyway, thinking there was no way that I could have possibly missed it. After another hour or more of driving south, I saw a big sign that said, "Welcome to Mexico." My thoughts raced, *What? NO way! I don't have the proper documents to present. I have no passport and I don't speak the language. Once I cross the gate, there is no way the INS officers will let me back in the States, and Maryl is at the babysitter!* Now I was completely panicked and frazzled because I didn't know how to get off the freeway. Then I decided I would get off on the closest off-ramp before it reached Mexico. As soon as I got off the freeway, I quickly found a gas station and showed the nice man who worked there the paper with my directions. He told me I needed to get back on the 5 freeway and head north; I was way off course. Feeling incredibly tense and overwhelmingly lost, I got back in my car and carefully followed the kind man's instructions. After what seemed like an eternity, I finally found my way back to Colorado Blvd. and managed to get to my new job at 12:30 p.m. Understandably, my cousin was really embarrassed because she had highly recommended me and I was late on my first day.

After I explained what had happened, she laughed at me and so did everyone who heard about my mishap. I guess I was supposed to know how to read the map. After that incident, I was jokingly referred to as being "fresh off the boat." I didn't really care because it was a lesson well learned. Eventually, I was introduced to my new boss and the rest of my fellow workers. When the day ended, my cousin told me to go on ahead of her and pick up the children because she needed to stay and work a bit later.

When I picked them up, I was so glad to see Maryl and the

boys. This time I had figured out how to get back home and realized the side streets were closer and faster. It only took us 30 minutes to get home. I made dinner for everyone when we got home. After the children ate, I cleaned the kitchen. While the boys stayed with their dad in the living room, Maryl and I went to our bedroom. As I was getting Maryl ready for bed, I asked her about her day and how things went for her. Maryl told me it was "fine" and said that she had fun playing with the boys. She mentioned that the lady was nice to her. I was overcome with relief.

Maryl and I stayed with my cousin for about two months. I did the daily routine of taking all three children to the sitter, then picking them up and cooking dinner for them. Sadly, things didn't work out as well as I had hoped. So one Sunday afternoon, Maryl and I suddenly dumped everything we had in my car and drove away. I was furious when we left because I felt dreadfully sorry about our situation. I was concerned about the impact on my daughter because she loved the boys, but I was emotionally tired and confused. Not having anywhere to go, I drove toward Colorado Blvd. in Glendale, California, because this was an area that was familiar and close to my job. I thought it would probably be convenient to stay in the area in order not to rush Maryl early in the morning. We promptly found a motel on Colorado Blvd. called the Comfort Inn, and I decided that we would reside there until something better came along. Our next step was to inform the INS agency of our move because they needed to know where we were at all times for our own safety.

As soon as I settled our bill and finished checking in at the front desk, Maryl and I went straight to our new room. She was so excited because the room was humongous as far as she was concerned. Our room had a king-sized bed, a small fridge, and our own microwave. We were all set! Our first task was to put all of our belongings away, and then I asked Maryl if she wanted to explore the area. It was crucial for us to learn where to buy inexpensive meals, and I needed to discover a place where she could be outside and play. Imagine our enthusiasm when we found a Thai restaurant right beside the motel. Thai food is a bit similar to Filipino food, and that is where we ate dinner that night. We immediately fell in love with the food, and it became one of our favorite restaurants. Maryl had chicken barbecue and rice, and I had the pork barbecue. We also drank their delicious Thai iced tea. Our bill was only $12, much to my delight. *What a great deal*, I thought. I was encouraged that this could really work.

We also found a McDonald's nearby, so I let her play for a little bit. Maryl enjoyed that after dinner and appeared to be totally care-free. It was comforting for me to realize while I watched her play that she clearly didn't really understand what had just happened and why we had to move so unexpectedly. She was just happy we were still together. All I wanted was to spare and protect Maryl from any pain and misery. We were also able to find a Catholic church down the street. When we saw it, I told her that we would start attending every Sunday, and she happily responded, "Okay." When Maryl finished playing and we had scouted our surroundings, we drove back to our motel room. I gave Maryl a quick bath so she could sleep in for a bit longer in the morning. After we both got ready for bed, we jumped onto our big bed, twirled around all over it, and proceeded to start a small pillow fight. Neither of us could believe how big our bed was. Because we had been sharing a small twin mattress on the floor for a while, this bed made us feel free and like we were "living large"! Sleeping peacefully that night, I was grateful for our new place.

Maryl was able to see her cousins every day because I continued taking her to the same babysitter. From the beginning of my job, for at least the first two weeks, I couldn't help but feel absolutely inadequate and stupid because the U.S. culture was extremely different. Literally, I was experiencing a major culture shock. For instance, it became apparently clear to me that the English that was taught in the Philippines was not really how people spoke in California. Whenever I said something, it felt like I only got a lot of "Huh?" or "What did you just say?" responses. Usually, that was followed by a look of confusion. Then people would burst into laughter, and I had no idea why. Also, I would ask, "Where is the comfort room?" and the person would appear totally perplexed. Then they would respond, "What now? Did you mean the restroom?" As far as I was concerned, the two terms mean the same thing, but apparently that wasn't the case.

My accent was a problem area too. I had always spoken English; that is our second language in the Philippines. We have 7,107 islands, and although there are indeed hundreds of dialects, there are 120 distinct languages. It was necessary to learn English for us to communicate with each other. I had been fortunate and was able to go to an excellent private school where the standard of education was outstanding. We were allowed to speak Tagalog only during Filipino subject, which was just an hour out of the eight hours of school per day. Then for the rest of the day we had to speak English.

One day when I asked one of my co-workers to provide me with an estimate for the job we were working on, she gave me a bewildered look and said, "You want a coat?" gesturing to a hanging coat jacket. I quickly responded, "No, a quote." We went back and forth with "quote" and "coat" for quite a few seconds before I realized I was pronouncing the word incorrectly. Although I was saying "coat," I really was meaning to say "quote." On another occasion, when a co-worker and I passed each other in the hallway, she looked at me and asked, "Hey, how are you doing?" Immediately, I started to tell her all about my day and how rough it had been. Much to my surprise, she interrupted me and said, "I don't really have time for this right now, so sorry" and then walked away. I stood there thinking to myself, *Then why did you even ask me?*

There were also American idioms such as, "Don't let the cat out of the bag" or "You made your bed; now lie in it." Whenever I tried to say these, they would come out completely distorted and messed up, like "You have a bed, now lie on it," or something of that sort, which gave people another reason to laugh at me. These experiences were totally humiliating for me and not fun at all. Therefore, I spent a lot of time observing and sincerely listening to what was happening around me. I especially paid particular attention to the way people would pronounce words as opposed to how I said them. It didn't take too long for me to figure out that one of the biggest problems I struggled with was the difference in the pronunciation of the letter "T." Filipinos would pronounce their "T" as a hard "T" as opposed to a soft "T," so to speak. It was challenging for me to learn not to say everything I was thinking. All too often, whatever I was thinking wasn't said properly, and somehow when I spoke, it sounded hurtful to people even though that wasn't my intention.

Here are two examples: Back home in the Philippines, it was okay and acceptable to say, "Your child is so fat; therefore, he/she is cute!" However, that was considered quite offensive here in the States. I once referred to the handicap parking spot as the "invalid space." The Tagalog language is very specific, literal, and straightforward. Now I can understand why those would be considered totally offensive to others. Back home, people were into each other's business, and this was considered by our culture to be acceptable and completely permissible. It's their way of letting one another know they care. The Filipino people are considered to be hospitable, generous, and compassionate. This is especially true for the people coming from the provinces and small towns.

On the other hand, Manila is very similar to the city of Los Angeles or even New York. The culture in Manila is so much more rushed with the daily hustle and bustle of life. But no matter how busy they are, Filipinos always find time to laugh, relax, and have "siesta time." All in all I managed to adjust to these cultural differences; in spite of the early challenges, it pretty much became easy over the course of time.

Chapter Eight

A Good Christmas, After All

After about a month at my job, I finally started to feel a little bit more comfortable. I began to learn to laugh with anyone who would laugh at my accent. I learned how to ask, "Is it okay to say..." or "How do you say..." or "What is the proper way of saying..." However, I definitely learned a great deal through this often-painful process. Although I was just a gofer at this job, I always dressed up coming to work and took extreme pride in whatever task I performed. Once in a while, someone would ask me if I was uncomfortable wearing such nice clothes to work when I just ran around all day and did menial jobs. My response would be to say a quick no, and then I would move on and not let their comments distract or discourage me. The two gentlemen who owned the marketing research company I worked for were a French man and an American. I really loved working for them because they were good men and always very kind to me. Eventually, I had to truthfully share with them some of the information regarding my history of working for the INS. Although I couldn't really tell them about Victor, they completely understood that at any time the INS could call me to work for them on the spot and I didn't have the luxury or option to say no. I was very thankful that they accepted this part of my life and were able to deal with my situation.

One of the most important parts of my job was to ship the data of tracking studies to any of the Fortune 500 companies we worked with. It was my responsibility to make in-house copies before I sent the original copies to the clients. One of our project directors asked me to ship two sets of tracking studies. These studies were for two of the top manufacturing car companies in the world. Let's just call them company A and company B. Before the project director left that night, she made sure that I completely understood that these two companies were in direct competition; therefore, it was essential that I made sure the studies were mailed out correctly.

As soon as I walked into the office the next morning, my immediate supervisor called me to his office. He solemnly informed me that I had made a very huge mistake the previous night. Apparently, the documents got mixed up and were sent to the wrong company when I shipped them. Although the envelopes were labeled correctly, somehow the data that was meant for company A went to company B and vice versa. Bottom line, both companies had received their direct competitor's data tracking study!

Immediately, I felt my face flush as I stood there in absolute shock. When I asked my boss what I could possibly do to help rectify this mix-up, he replied, "This is the kind of mistake people get fired for, and the project director wants me to fire you immediately. I am so sorry." *Just like that? I am fired?* I thought to myself. *Now what am I going to do? I can't afford to lose this job, especially now.* My mind was trying to process what just happened. I asked if he could please beg her for my job back, and he simply said, "Nope, I will not go against that woman's decision." At that point I decided I would beg for my job. My immediate supervisor tried to stop me, but I bolted out of his office. I walked up to the second floor and went straight to the project director's office. The door was shut, and when I knocked on it, I could tell I startled her. When I asked if I could speak with her for a moment, she reluctantly said yes. Once I stood in front of her desk, I found myself struggling not to cry and to keep my composure.

I said to her, "I know the mistake I made was unforgivable, and if I were not a single mother with a 3-year-old, I would not be here pleading with you to keep my job. But I am begging you; please, I need this job to support my daughter. Please give me another chance. If I make another mistake, you won't have to fire me; I will quit." I wasn't sure what she was thinking, but she looked me in the eyes and said, "Okay." After I thanked her and started to walk away, I could feel my knees go completely weak. I went directly to the restroom, and as the door closed, I burst into tears.

That was the last time I ever made a mistake. As a result of what happened, I developed an excessive orderliness and became extremely meticulous. I implemented a 4:30 p.m. deadline for myself for all copies to be made and had a 5:00 p.m. deadline if no copies were necessary. Despite my circumstances, I kept my spirits high and continued to work very hard. On slow days, I would walk around to check which departments needed help, and then I would lend a hand.

I did this for two specific reasons: first, because I hated to sit around and not do anything. When I became idle, it caused me to get bored and I felt useless. Second, I wanted to understand all aspects of the marketing research world. The owners of the company used to walk around the building to check and see how their workers were doing. Oftentimes, the French owner would see me working with various employees in different departments. At one point, he even asked one of the managers if I had been moved to another department. He thought it was a good idea that I tried to find work in another department when business was slow for me, and he appreciated my work ethic. Both of the owners became very fond of me and respected my dedication to their company. They would often comment about the way I was always dressed up for work. They both said it showed that I loved what I did and valued their company no matter what department I worked in.

Once in a while, the INS would call me to work on an assignment, but nothing was as big as the Mabuhay case. Sometimes all I had to do was translate Tagalog into English or have a meeting with the "crook" and pose as an illegal alien who needed a visa. The latter was a bit uncomfortable for me, but the INS always placed agents somewhere I could see them. Plus, as much as I hated doing these jobs, it did provide extra income for Maryl and me because I got compensated for my work. They paid me according to what the job was and depending on how involved I was in the case.

On one day in particular, Agent Jimenez called me and asked if I would meet with him and Agent Price for lunch. He proceeded to tell me that he had something important for me. I made plans with them to meet at a restaurant by my work. I was feeling unbelievably anxious on my way to the restaurant because I didn't really want to do any CI work so close to Christmas. When I arrived at the designated meeting place, Jimenez and Price were already there, and they greeted me with a huge smile. When I sat down, they politely asked me what I wanted to eat for lunch. Because I wasn't really hungry and my stomach was in knots, I just ordered coffee. Before they had a chance to say anything, the first words I blurted out were, "What's the assignment?" Jimenez immediately responded, "There is no assignment; we wanted to present to you, on behalf of the Immigration and Naturalization Service, a plaque of appreciation for the success of the Mabuhay case. It's for your hard work and your willingness to help us put Victor away. In addition to this plaque comes $2,500. It's not much, but we thought you and your daughter could have a nice Christmas."

Needless to say, I was completely dumbfounded, and I didn't really know what to say. They could tell I was very happy and totally overwhelmed. I felt appreciated and finally felt like I was a real person, not an illegal alien! Jimenez told me he brought a Polaroid camera and asked if I would like to have my picture taken with my plaque of appreciation. "Absolutely!" I exclaimed. We all went outside the restaurant to pose and asked a bystander to take our picture. Jimenez gave me the picture, and they left. I stood there holding my Polaroid picture, my award, and my cash! I was singing on my way back to work and felt like I was floating. That afternoon, as soon as I picked up Maryl I told her the good news. At 5 years old, she didn't really have much to say until I told her that we would have a nice dinner and then she could shop and pick out a Barbie doll of her choice. That seemed to make her night, and she was excited about our good fortune.

Thank God I had Maryl to share my joy with because I couldn't really tell anybody else. I was able to tell her I got an award for my hard work and for doing a good job. She responded, "I am glad you did a good job, Mommy." "Thanks, Maryl, it looks like we will have a nice Christmas after all," I said. At this point it had been a whole month since we moved into the Comfort Inn motel. The weekends were kind of tough for Maryl because she didn't have a playmate, and it was lonely. Maryl always acted like she didn't seem to mind, but as her mother, I felt that she was probably missing an essential part of her childhood not living in a neighborhood where she had friends. We always ran errands and did our laundry on Saturdays. On Sunday mornings, we would go to the Catholic Church around the corner. I especially loved the woman who would sing solos. I loved the way she sang "As the Deer," and it was one of my favorite worship songs at church. Maryl never wanted to go to the children's Sunday school. Instead, she was simply content to stay with me. I didn't mind at all because she was so well behaved and quiet during service that no one even knew she was there.

Our Sunday ritual also included going to lunch at the Lamplighter restaurant in Glendale after church. Then I would take Maryl to McDonald's so she could play in the moon bounce with all the other children who were there. By three in the afternoon, we would head back to our motel. We would both lay around on our king-sized bed and talk and laugh. I usually told her stories that would normally take quite a while to finish because Maryl repeatedly interrupted with so many of her insightful questions. At this point, Maryl was very fluent in English and barely spoke Tagalog. I would always tell her not to forget how to speak Tagalog.

It was important to me that she knew her origin and was proud to be a Filipino. I usually scolded her in English first and then again in Tagalog. The poor girl would literally get a double scolding. However, this was my way of reinforcing our native language. Interestingly, Maryl never asked about her biological father. It's not because I ever denied his existence. The reality was that she just never seemed to care. Sometimes I would ask her if she missed him, and she would always quickly respond by saying no. It wasn't until quite a bit later that I learned her first memory of her biological father. It was when she was just barely 3 years old. Maryl remembers him roughly shoving her inside the bathroom where it was totally dark with all the lights off. It grieves me that she clearly recalls being so scared in the dark bathroom alone. She can still remember fumbling around blindly while she was in there and yelling out for me to come help her. Regrettably, I also remembered that day and will never forget it either. Her biological father had come to visit. Maryl was unusually cranky that day. I had to go upstairs to get something and left her nanny to look after her. As soon as I left, she started to cry uncontrollably, and this irritated her father to the point of finally locking her in the dark bathroom. When I heard her yelling, I immediately ran downstairs and cursed at him for being so cruel to her. This only caused me to hate him even more.

An Indecent Woman

🌸

There was a time when I actually thought I was in love with him. When I met him, he reminded me so much of my dad. He had all the qualities that I admired most in my dad. He was incredibly smart, was very generous, had a wonderful sense of humor, and dressed impeccably. The Chinese-Filipino-born woman I was renting from introduced him to me. At that time, I was only 19 years old. This woman had a son and a sister who also lived with us. She was a tall, charming lady with porcelain-like skin and a jovial personality, and she was a smart businesswoman. When I first met them, she and her sister were dating military men from Sangley Point. This used to be an American air base and was located in Cavite. Neither of the sisters knew how to drive. Therefore, I would drive them to the base so they could visit with their boyfriends. It was almost a two-hour drive. When we finally arrived, they would both take off and then I would just wait for them until their rendezvous was over.

Because she gave me a great rate on my rent, I would reciprocate by driving for them whenever they needed me. It was usually once a week. Occasionally their boyfriends came down to Manila, and it was during one of those unique times that I was introduced to a high-ranking officer of the Philippine Air Force. He was at least 20 years my senior and introduced himself as a widower. It wasn't until much later that I found out he was actually still married and had six children; Maryl eventually became his seventh child, at least as far as I know. The Major's (his rank at the time) family lived in Cavite, and my family resided in Manila. Because that was such a significant distance, it made his story about being widowed seem plausible. I never really understood why no one ever told me that he wasn't really a widower. Without a doubt, I also wanted to believe him.

I so strongly craved the attention and kindness that he lavished upon me. I particularly liked the fact that he was a very generous person, and not just with me. Quite often I observed his generosity that frequently extended to the less fortunate. I sincerely admired this quality about him. He was kindhearted and good to the people who were important to me, like my family. When I later found out he was actually married, I felt an enormous sense of guilt, and then I made a deal with God. It was in one of those conversations with God that I asked Him to please forgive me. I confessed my love for this man and truly thought it was far too late for me to back out of this relationship. I asked God if He would cut me some slack by allowing me to continue in my relationship with him; I promised God that in return I would never bother his family, and I definitely would never ask him to leave them for me.

When I was a month pregnant, I moved out of the house owned by the two sisters and ended up sharing a three-bedroom house with two couples. I was renting one of the bedrooms, but by the time I reached my second trimester, the Major thought I should move to my own place. He found an apartment close to Villamor Air Base where he was stationed. By now I had realized that his entire family had moved from Cavite to the military base. My apartment was fully furnished; I had one female help and one Private-ranking military man living with me. I treated them like family. The three of us would regularly eat together at the dinner table. They kept me company and watched over me.

It was during this time that my own family, specifically Grandma Lola, couldn't understand why I ever chose to become the mistress of a married man. Unfortunately, my grandmother was exactly right. There really was no excuse for my behavior during that season. Without a doubt, I knew I was doing something wrong, but I was very tired of moving from one place to another.

After I was raped at age 13, I felt like a "used car," like "damaged goods." I truly believed in my heart that no decent man would ever want to marry someone like me. This was also part of my Filipino culture back then. No man would bring a woman like me to meet his mother. I simply resigned myself to what I felt I had become, an indecent woman. I did everything in my power to make sure I was not interfering with the Major's family. I panicked when he was rushed to the hospital for an emergency surgery, yet I forced myself to not go near him. Although I really wanted to see him, I unquestionably knew that I couldn't. During that time, I had no idea what was happening to him, and I was worried about what was going to happen to my unborn child and me. As expected, I kept thinking, What if this is serious and he dies? What would happen to me then? As it turned out, the Major had a benign cyst. He always came and visited me whenever he felt like it. Yet whenever he didn't want to visit me, I never called or bothered him. I understood and accepted that I had no right whatsoever.

When it was time for me to give birth, I drove myself to the hospital. I was two weeks past my due date, and the doctor was getting worried. He told me they would have to induce labor, but if that didn't work, I may need to have a C-section. I immediately prayed to God and asked Him to not allow that to happen, primarily because I knew the recovery would be so much slower, and I didn't have anyone to take care of me. No one in my family knew I was at the hospital. During my labor, the Major was in Cavite for a cockfight derby. This was one of his favorite sports and pastimes. He was also very fond of the casino. He actually won quite often, and when he did, *he would always give me some money.*

He also really liked women. During this time, women were often given to him as a gift from the high-ranking officials. This was their way of building rapport, and it made business deals move more quickly. Because the Major was considered the right hand of the General at the Air Base, he was frequently lavished upon with gifts. I never really knew about all the other women, until one acquaintance came over to see me. While we were visiting, she swore to me that she had seen the Major early that afternoon at the Manila Peninsula Hotel with a very young woman. That same evening, the Major came to my house when I was about seven months pregnant. As soon as he walked in, I questioned him about the girl. He tried to deny it for quite a while, but I must have eventually driven him to the point of exhaustion because he yelled back, "Yes, it's true!"

As soon as I heard these words from his mouth, I felt totally defeated. I couldn't even begin to reconcile in my mind why he would need to be with some other woman, especially this one. The pain was so devastating; I honestly wished that he had just continued to deny everything. I thought about how much his wife would hurt if she ever found out about us. After that confession, things were never the same for me ever again. The dynamics of our relationship changed dramatically.

Suddenly I realized there really was no guarantee that he would take care of my child and me. From that point on, I started to save all my money. Every single penny he gave me, I saved. The Major volunteered to put a CD aside for Maryl's future. Although it wasn't that much, it was definitely a good start. I decided to go to school where I learned how to make curtains. I chose this course because it was something I could do out of my own home, and it was my own business. When I asked the Major to help me win the contract for replacing the curtains at the Air Base, he willingly gave it to me. This was such a big deal because I made 65 percent profit and was able to save all of it. Then I went to school to study cosmetology because someone told me this career was in large demand in the United States. I also took a sales job in Makati for a few months. During this time I met my best friend, Stella, and her family. I eventually stopped caring for the Major, who by now was promoted to a colonel, especially knowing what he had done.

Amidst all these changes, I added a new petition to the "Mother of Perpetual Help" in Baclaran. This time, I was asking her to help me give Maryl a better life by allowing us to leave for the United States. I tried to leave the Philippines for the States legally. However, the U.S. Immigration automatically denied my petition upon realizing that my dad was a U.S. citizen who had already filed a petition for his children to come to the States. When that attempt proved futile, my next option was to apply for Canadian citizenship, but this also was to no avail. I had spent a significant part of my savings during these processes, but I didn't really care. I had a goal and was determined to accomplish it no matter what the cost. Of course, it was in the midst of this time of searching for ways to get to the United States that I stumbled upon Manuel, who agreed to illegally help me, and that eventually led to the Mabuhay case.

In retrospect, it was clearly a blessing to have learned about the other women in the Major's life because that fact truly woke me up to a harsh reality. I realized the Major was not my savior. He didn't save me from ruin; he was merely taking advantage of my poor self-esteem. I started to gain hope and believed that I could change my life and lead a life of decency. Even when Maryl and I ended up living in a motel, we were still better off without him in our life. We could look forward to a better and bright future together.

Maryl and I had been staying at the Comfort Inn motel for almost a month and a half when dad's ex-wife called. This was not my mom and not the stepmother who was currently living with my dad; this was another woman. My dad had a son with her, which makes him my half brother. I was happy to hear from her, especially when she offered to rent us her extra bedroom for only $300 a month, which included all utilities. Without hesitating, I said yes right away and then told Maryl the good news. It only took us an hour to pack everything we owned. We moved from the motel to her home on Vermont Street in Los Angeles. It was an old, Tudor-style house that was very clean and well kept. All of the neighbors were very nice to us. As a matter of fact, one of the neighbors ended up babysitting Maryl. The sitter had two little girls whom Maryl loved.

We were at this same house when Maryl turned 5 years old. We held her birthday party on a Saturday to have a good turnout, but because we were so new in the neighborhood, we didn't know any children to invite. So Maryl only had one guest who was her age, and the rest of our guests were my co-workers. I made plenty of Filipino food, cake, and ice cream. My associates loved the Filipino food, and that made me real happy. Maryl received a lot of gifts, and everyone treated her very kindly. They paid attention to her during the entire party. Each person took turns talking to her individually, and they made sure she felt extra-special that birthday. Fortunately, I was the only person in our company who had a child, which meant everyone was especially nice to Maryl and me.

A few months later, I received a surprising phone call from the Colonel. He informed me that he was making a trip to the United States. Apparently, he belonged to the Fil-American golf tournament, and they were scheduled to compete here. When he asked if he could come see Maryl, I said yes for Maryl's sake.

Then I asked my roommate, who was also my landlady, if he could stay with us for four days while he spent time with Maryl. She was kind to agree to this arrangement. I had no intentions of reviving my relationship with him, so I made sure he slept on Maryl's bed and that Maryl and I slept on my bed. Also, I kept our bedroom door open during the night because I didn't want him to get any ideas. When I announced to Maryl that the Colonel was coming to see her, she didn't really have much to say. This was understandable because she didn't really have a close relationship with him. He arrived on a Thursday, and because I had to go to work, I left Maryl home with him so they could spend time together. When I got home that evening, he asked me if we would travel with him to Dana Point near San Diego to visit one of his daughters who was married to a military man stationed there. I was adamantly against this idea because I was afraid our visit would hurt his daughter's feelings. The Colonel assured me that I would have nothing to worry about because she already knew all about Maryl. I wasn't quite sure about the whole concept, but the only thing I could think about was Maryl's opportunity to meet her half sister, so I finally agreed to the trip.

When we arrived, his daughter was very kind and gracious to us. She seemed genuinely happy to meet Maryl and me. I wasn't really sure why; maybe she was afraid of her dad. We had several shallow conversations about life, particularly her life. Although it felt very awkward and uncomfortable for me, she honestly didn't seem bothered by the situation at all, and that was really confusing to me. I mostly tried to steer the conversation back to talking about Maryl. When evening came, his daughter came up to me and explained the sleeping arrangement; she was giving me a room to share with her dad. I explained to her in a very nice way that it would not be necessary because I had no intentions of continuing any relationship with her father. Rather, this trip was strictly for Maryl's benefit. When I finished, she seemed very surprised about what I had shared with her. Therefore, I can only assume her father had told her something completely different, which would have been typical for him.

That night I couldn't sleep much. It was mainly because I was so uncomfortable. I honestly didn't know if I had done the right thing by bringing Maryl and introducing her to her half sister. I sincerely felt that I should never deny Maryl of the opportunity to meet her biological father, regardless of the history. I had decided to give Maryl the fair opportunity to get to know him and develop whatever type of relationship she felt comfortable with her father.

This was my firm conviction. I also made a vow to make sure that Maryl knew the truth about my life and honestly understood who I was. I would accomplish this by telling her various stories about my childhood. It was my strategic plan to do this incrementally, in ways that would be age-appropriate, of course.

For me, I grew up believing that my dad destroyed our family and he was entirely at fault. But as I got older and wiser, I realized it always takes two to make a marriage work. Be that as it may, Maryl should always know the truth. I didn't want her to end up like me. At this point of my life, I had lost every inch of faith, hope, and trust in people.

When we got up the next morning, the Colonel decided we could all go to Sea World. I intentionally planned on giving Maryl plenty of space and time to bond with her biological father. I watched them walk hand in hand, and when Maryl wanted her face painted, he quickly agreed and willingly paid for it. Even though I was very happy for Maryl, deep inside of me, I was truly worried about how she would be impacted when it was time for the Colonel to go back home to the Philippines. We started to head back to Los Angeles late that afternoon, and it came time for him to leave. I overheard Maryl asking him where he was going and why he couldn't stay with us. To be honest, it broke my heart to hear her pleading for her father to stay longer. He assured her that he would give her a call the following day before he boarded his plane for the Philippines.

When he left that night, Maryl was brokenhearted. Although she didn't cry, I could see it on her face. I blamed myself for what I had done to her and hated the fact I had allowed this to happen. I also felt guilty for destroying her life. How could I have chosen to bring up a child in this world and have her experience the pain she was going through? I saw myself as a selfish person who didn't think about the consequences of my behavior and decisions in life. I called Maryl from the doorway and gave her a big hug as I said, "Don't worry. Your dad will be back to see you again, maybe next year, okay?" She looked at me but kept completely silent. I decided to distract her by asking her to start getting ready for her shower, but I was taken aback when I heard her say no. She spoke with a defiant attitude that I had never seen before. "What did you just say to me?" I asked. Then Maryl responded, "No! I don't want you! I want to go live with my dad!" At that moment I didn't know what to say or how to respond.

I could feel anger rise within me. In addition, so many thoughts were rushing through my head that I had difficulty thinking clearly. I couldn't believe that a 5-year-old little girl could have such blatant disrespect. I was in complete disbelief, and I remember thinking, *I risked my life for this little brat?* I tried to brace myself as I responded to her in a very calm manner, "Well, if you would rather live with your dad, then it is okay with me. I would never want you to be where you don't want to be." I pulled out a big bag and started packing her clothes. "I will dial your dad's phone number, and I want you to ask him to come pick you up right now."

At this point my heart was pounding so fast because I was really afraid that Maryl would leave me for good to live with her dad. She was my life, and the thought of her leaving me for the Colonel felt like someone was physically ripping my heart out. However, I couldn't make her want to stay with me; it had to be her choice. If I begged her to stay, then she would end up manipulating me for the rest of her life, and I definitely couldn't allow that to happen. I decided it would be best for both of us to get this over with now, instead of dealing with it later. I was concerned that maybe the United States was not the best place to raise children. However, I had decided that I would rather lose her now than watch her destroy her life later on. I was so relieved when Maryl started to cry and said, "No, Mommy, I am sorry; I don't want to go! Please don't call him. I will take a shower now." I almost wanted to break down and cry with relief but managed to keep my composure.

I forced myself to ask her, "Are you sure, Maryl? Your dad is leaving tomorrow morning, so this may be your last chance to go with him." Much to my relief, she said, "Yes, I am sure, Mommy; I don't want to go." These were the sweetest words to my ears; I was so thankful.

Chapter Nine

Run As Fast As You Can

Shortly after the colonel's visit, Maryl and I had to move out of the house on Vermont Street. The environment had become inappropriate to raise a child, at least in my opinion. There was gambling going all day, and at times, it ran into the night. One day Maryl called me at work crying because my roommate instructed her to stay inside our bedroom because apparently, she bothered the gambling session. I was enraged upon hearing this so I asked my boss to let me off early that day. I was literally fuming while I drove 90 miles an hour to get to Maryl. When I got to the house, I barged into my roommate's room and said all the curse words I could think of. That night, Maryl and I moved out of the house and stayed with one of my friends from work until I could find us a place to live.

This presented a new challenge for me because Maryl was about to start first grade. The place I found for us to live was in North Hollywood, and I worked across town off of Colorado Blvd. in Los Angeles. Although Victor was still in jail, I had no desire to put Maryl in a school that I couldn't get to her in a matter of minutes. Consequently, I decided to put her in a public school right down the street from where I worked.

The after-school daycare was in the park, across from the building where I worked. This gave me such great peace of mind to know she was easily within my reach. One of my biggest fears during this time of my life was that I was afraid of dying because I had no one to leave Maryl with in case something ever happened to me. In my mind, no one would ever be able to love her and care for her as much as I did. On weekdays, we would leave our apartment at 7:00 a.m. because Maryl had to be in school. This meant we didn't have time to eat breakfast. I pre-paid her lunch for the whole week of school, so I didn't think about eating before we left in the morning. I imagined she would get hungry later in the morning during their snack time. Then one day when I picked her up from daycare, the worker told me that the lady in charge said Maryl ate too much! Her comment was offensive to me, and I became so angry that I confronted her.

Later, I realized Maryl got hungrier than other kids do because she didn't eat breakfast, and I never even packed a snack for her. I actually didn't realize that the food I paid for at her school only covered the lunch meal and nothing else. She had to wait until after-school daycare to get a snack. And she never even complained to me about feeling hungry. From that point on, I gave her extra money to be able to buy snacks at school and daycare.

More often than not, I would have to work overtime. Because I was paid hourly, the only way I could make additional income for us was to work the extra hours. Whenever possible, I specifically took advantage of the double-time pay. When I had to work late, I would pick up Maryl around 5:00 p.m. Then we would drive through McDonald's, and she always wanted the kid's meal. She particularly liked the different toys that came in the box with the meal. Maryl would always ask me to check the toy box immediately to ensure that I didn't get a duplicate. Whenever I took Maryl to my office, she did exactly what I asked her to do. I would say, "Maryl, sit here and do your homework; when you're done, I will give you papers and pens to write with." "Okay, Mommy," she would respond compliantly.

My entire office knew Maryl well. They were all amazingly nice to her, especially the two owners of the company. They even offered to put a couch by my cubicle for Maryl to sleep on when she came with me and got too tired. I usually worked until about 9:00 p.m., so it was quite a long day for both of us. Sometimes I ended up working there until 11:00 p.m. Maryl would be fast asleep most of the time, so I would just carry her from the car to our bed. Those long evenings made it very difficult for her to get up the next morning. In spite of the difficulty, it was necessary because we still needed the extra money.

During this time, our rent was $700 for a one-bedroom apartment, my car payment was $215 plus insurance, and that didn't even include our food and the normal necessities for each day. We barely managed financially because I was only making a mere $9.00 an hour.

Sadly, there were those occasional times when, after paying all of our bills, there was very little money left for food. Whenever this would happen, I would buy two dozen eggs and cook them in every way imaginable. I would cook scrambled eggs, scrambled with tomatoes and onions (this was her most favorite), egg salad, sunny-side up eggs, fried eggs, eggs over easy, hard-boiled eggs, and don't forget poached eggs. We literally ate eggs and rice for weeks until my next paycheck, but Maryl never seemed to know the difference. I sure didn't want her to know how difficult things were because I didn't want her to have a "self-pity," "poor me" attitude.

I also didn't want for her to develop any insecurity. This was the primary reason why we never utilized the government food stamps, even though we more than qualified. I thought those were only for people who were indigent. Sometimes Maryl and I would splurge by eating at the Rusty Pelican restaurant right by my work. They had a happy hour that also provided great food. You could purchase 10 shrimp for a dollar! They also offered three taquitos or a quesadilla for a dollar. We would get to the restaurant bar at exactly 5:00 p.m. because I wanted to get Maryl out of there before all the patrons arrived for their drinks. We would sit at our own table, and because the restaurant was pretty fancy-looking, Maryl thought we were living large. She would be so excited, and I can still remember her asking me, "Mommy, can I have more shrimps after this?" Because this was one of her favorite foods, she would eat a lot. I can even remember asking her to eat her food fast so she could have as much as she wanted before people came to drink and we had to leave. We couldn't take any of the food to go with us, so we had to sit and eat it all right there. I would always order a soda for me and get an orange juice for Maryl so the restaurant would let us sit there and eat the special food they had for only a dollar to accompany our drinks.

One day in particular, I was able to leave my office at exactly 5:00 p.m. I picked up Maryl from her daycare and told her we needed to stop by Rite Aid to pick up a few things. She liked going to the store with me because she was allowed to pick one thing she wanted, with the exception of chewing gum. I have always told her that it isn't ladylike to chew gum.

She wasn't allowed to eat or buy candies either, so Maryl would usually pick out inexpensive toys that only cost a dollar. I parked the car right across from Rite Aid and not too far from the entrance door. As Maryl and I were walking toward the entrance, an old Volkswagen van stopped right in front of us. The man driving the van was obviously staring at me, I couldn't help but notice. He had a smile on his face, so I smiled back at him and remember thinking to myself, *I know this man, but I can't remember from where.*

Then just as soon as the van passed by me, I realized that the man who was smiling at me was none other than Victor! I immediately began to panic. *Is he out of jail? But how can that be when it hasn't even been five years yet?* I tried to calm myself down as thoughts raced rapidly through my head. I had to convince myself to keep my composure and then considered the possibility that if he turned back around to park his van and followed me into the store, it would definitely be Victor. Maryl and I continued to walk into the store, and as soon as we got there, we hid behind the glass door. I tried to look for the van, but it was nowhere in sight. At this point, I thought maybe I was just plain paranoid. I let out a huge sigh and decided to move on and begin my shopping.

We proceeded to pick up a half-gallon of milk, a cup of noodle soup that we found on sale for only a dollar, several cans of spam, and a dozen eggs. Maryl bought herself a Yan-Yan. I was pleased with our choices and figured these things would last us for about a week or so until my next paycheck. We proceeded to the checkout stand that was open, and I started to unload our items from our cart. When I looked up, there was Victor standing directly behind the lady checker who was ringing up our groceries and near the place where the bags were situated. Although I immediately recognized Victor and positively knew it was him, I continued under the pretense that I did not recognize him. "Hi," he said, looking directly at me. "Hi," I retorted with a friendly smile on my face. I tried to avoid looking at him directly because I knew he would sense that I was truly very scared. I wasn't sure how long he was actually standing right there in front of me, although it seemed like a long while.

The next time I looked up to pay for my groceries, he had disappeared! *Oh my God, where did he go now?* I thought. My heart started to pound as the harsh reality hit me that Victor had just stood directly in front of Maryl and me and spoke to me. I grabbed my groceries, and I talked to Maryl in a calm voice as we were leaving the store. Fortunately my voice did not reflect the panic I was fighting. Calmly I said, "We're going to play a game, okay, Maryl? I am going to count from one to three, and when I get to three, you are going to run as fast as Mommy does, get into your car seat, and buckle up really, really fast, okay?" "Okay," she said with a big smile on her face. Maryl was oblivious to the danger we were both facing, and I was grateful she was still naïve.

As we got closer to the store's automatic door, I started to count, "One, two, three!" And we both ran as fast as we could, holding hands, to our car. I quickly opened her car door first. "Buckle up now, Maryl!" I reminded her. Then I ran to the driver's side, got into the car, buckled up, started the car, and immediately maneuvered as fast as I could out of the parking lot. When I looked in the rearview mirror, I was horrified to realize that there was Victor in his beat-up VW van right behind us! I was supposed to take the 170 freeway north to drive home, but I took the 2 freeway north instead. Under no circumstance could I go home directly, and I absolutely needed to lose him.

I wasn't sure what Maryl was thinking about, and she was unusually quiet while we drove. She didn't even ask any questions during our drive. I think she could sense that something was terribly wrong. I kept thinking to myself that Victor was probably going to torture me first, before he proceeded to kill me because of the time he had spent in jail. I was completely petrified by the very thought of him getting near Maryl. Already, I had been driving for two miles, and he was still right behind us. Interestingly, because I was driving 95 miles an hour, for the first time in my life, I was praying that a police officer would pull me over for speeding, but there was not one in sight. *Where are they when you need them?* I thought.

I switched lanes rapidly to take the 134 freeway and continued to speed. Still there were no police officers anywhere to be found, and I had no idea of where I should drive now. When I looked up again, he was gone. It must have been about another three miles or so that he was able to follow us before I had lost him. God was surely watching over Maryl and me because Victor happened to be driving a beat-up VW van. Had it been his brand-new Mercedes-Benz, we wouldn't have had a chance. My knees were still shaking. I wasn't convinced that we had really lost him and didn't know if he was still behind us hiding somewhere out of sight. I slowed down a little bit, and when I was sure he was really gone, I looked for a telephone booth to make a call. "Forman" was the response that I heard on the second ring. I cannot even begin to explain how reassuring it was to hear his voice again. My throat was dry and I knew my voice was cracking when I blurted out, "Victor found us and was following us. I just lost him on the freeway, but what should I do? Please help us, Forman. Is he out of jail now? Why didn't you tell me? Well, is he out?" By now I was yelling at him on the other line.

Forman tried to stay calm and replied, "Yes, Corinna, he got out two months ago for his good behavior. We didn't tell you because we didn't want to worry you. If you are certain that he is not following you anymore, I need for you and Maryl to go home, and we will be there before you get there." I told him okay and then hung up the phone. I was still shaking when I got back into my car and drove home with Maryl. I was so confused and scared I didn't even know what to do, and I couldn't think clearly at all. When we got to the house, I locked the doors and windows and kept Maryl right beside me the whole time. I kept thinking of ways that I could defend us if he had followed us back to our house. I went to the kitchen to see if I could find a sharp knife. I was looking for an escape route in case Victor came through our front door. Unfortunately, it was the only way out for us because we lived on the second floor and there were no stairs available, only a window.

A loud knock startled me, and I heard, "This is Forman; open the door." As soon as I saw him, I was relieved and felt safer. Then my emotions totally flipped, and I started to get angry with him. I told him that it wasn't right for them to keep this information from me because I was caught defenseless and was left totally unaware of the huge change in circumstances. Here I was thinking my daughter and I were still safe because according to my information, Victor was supposedly still behind bars. How could he ever get out on good behavior? I thought he was found guilty on five counts! Didn't they tell me that it would be five years behind bars, not three, for Victor based on good behavior? Forman stood there quietly and didn't really have much to say. In all honesty, he knew there was nothing he could say to make the situation better for me at that moment, and so he allowed me to totally vent my frustration.

I asked him, "What am I supposed to do now?" Forman told me in a very matter-of-fact manner that Maryl and I could not continue to live in the house that we were at, and we had no choice but to move right away. He also said that the INS officers were downstairs and would not leave until tomorrow morning. Then he asked me if I had ever used a gun. He offered to give me a gun to protect us from Victor until we were moved and relocated from our house. However, I refused without any hesitation.

Nowhere to Go

❀

There was only one time I had "used" a gun. One day, the Colonel pushed me down hard on the bed, climbed on top of me, held both my hands, and slapped me with both the back of his hand and then forehand style. He hit me so hard that I literally saw twinkling stars and my ears started ringing incessantly. I was in total shock and unable to move for a few minutes, but when I regained enough strength to move, I grabbed his .357 Magnum and pointed it right at him. Then I told the Colonel, as I aimed the gun toward him, "If you ever touch me again, I am going to kill you and I mean it!" Needless to say, he left my house very quickly that day. I made an immovable decision; that was the first and the last time he or any man would ever hurt me again. My Grandma Lola used to tell me, "If you ever let a man hit you once and you let it go, he will do it over and over again. Take care to resolve it the first time it happens." I knew she was right and took heed of my grandma's advice for myself. Yet I remember witnessing my mom's boyfriend, whom she eventually ended up marrying, beat her very badly.

After my dad left us, my mom started drinking, which ultimately led to her alcoholism. Watching her drink to the point of losing herself was a normal occurrence in our house. I was so young and knew nothing about the disease of alcohol. My mom was a very beautiful woman; Filipinos referred to her as a "mestiza." This was because her Spaniard features were very prominent. Most Filipino women are usually short in height, but my mom, standing 5 feet 5 inches tall, wasn't the norm. She had fair skin, deep dark-set eyes, and dark brown hair, and her nose had a pretty high bridge. She definitely stood out in a crowd. There were so many men who would do anything just to get her attention, and it has always been mind-boggling to me that she liked this particular man and chose him above others.

They were both functioning alcoholics. She and her boyfriend held pretty decent jobs during the day, but it was when they got home or whenever there were occasions to celebrate that they would get drunk. Frequently, the later the night got, the more drama there would be in our home. Usually this consisted of crying, yelling, and throwing or breaking things around the house. One night, just like any other night, I was trying to get some sleep by burying my head under my pillows. I heard a loud thud, and my mom let out a cry that was different than I had ever heard before. I was forced to come out of my room very quickly and, right at that moment, caught her boyfriend kicking her in the stomach while she was desperately gasping for her breath. I became very angry by the sight before me. I ran to our kitchen where I grabbed the sharpest knife I could find. I stepped right between my mom, who was lying on the floor holding her stomach in pain, and her boyfriend's foot, which was about to kick her again.

I stood there yelling for him to stop and pointed the blade directly at his face. I was a very young teenager at the time, skinny and short in stature, but I could tell he was completely taken aback by my behavior. I demanded him to step away from my mom or I would cut his face. Much to my surprise, he did back off. My mom quickly sobered up and then proceeded to try to protect her boyfriend from me. She spoke to me in an angry manner and yelled at me to go to my room and to stop interfering in their personal argument. Needless to say, I was very confused at her reaction because I couldn't understand why she was protecting him from me. It appeared that all of a sudden she was magically sober and everything was okay. I swiftly dropped the knife and went back to my room. I felt desperately confused and unable to comprehend what had just happened. This time I buried my face on my pillow so no one could hear my sobs. When I got up the next morning, my mom and her boyfriend both acted like nothing even happened the night before.

Later my mom called for me to come out of my room and sat me down. She said, "Corinna, next time don't you ever, ever interfere in my business again!" Because I was raised to not ever talk back, I responded in a polite tone, "Are you asking me to watch him kick you and say nothing?" This whole concept stunned me and seemed unrealistic. She emphatically continued, "Yes, that is exactly what I am asking you to do! Remember, it's none of your business!" Without saying another word, I went to my room and started to cry again. I was careful because I didn't want her to know that she had hurt my feelings. Still on guard, I quickly wiped all my tears away and started to pack my things pretending to leave. Because I really didn't have anywhere to go, deep inside I was frantically hoping she would come in and try to stop me and we would talk things over. Undoubtedly, I was very wrong and had totally underestimated the situation. Instead of her fixing the situation between us, when she saw me packing, she yelled from across the living room, "If you leave this house now, don't you ever come back again. Do you hear me?" My response to her was simply, "Yes, I heard you, and I would never come back." So I never did.

When I walked out of her house, I purposefully walked very slowly, hoping against hope that she would call me back to say she didn't mean what she said and then make me come back inside the house. I must have been walking for about a mile before I realized that no one was coming to stop me and no one cared or worried what would happen to me. Upon that full realization, I started sobbing. My tears were mainly because I felt completely alone. I was beginning to grasp the fact that I had no money and literally didn't know where to go. After standing in a shaded public transportation stop area for hours, I decided the safest place for me to go was the Malate church. Once again, I was going to pray and ask God to help me.

I had actually found the Malate church by accident. Sometime after my parents separated, my mom and I moved back in with my Grandma Lola. I was about 12 years old. It was one of those days my grandma was very angry with my mom for not coming home regularly. My mom explained to my grandma that the distance between her workplace and where we lived made it very difficult and dangerous to travel every single night. She further clarified that it cost so much money to commute. "So where are you staying every evening?" asked Grandma. "I am renting a room with a girlfriend in Malate. It's right beside the Malate church, 15 minutes away from where I work. Do not worry; I will be home on Friday nights and not leave until Sunday so I can spend time with Corinna," my mom responded. I have never been sure, but truthfully I think my mom thought she would score points for telling my grandma that where she was staying was beside a church.

In the beginning, my mom was true to her word. Every Friday afternoon, I would sit by the window of our bedroom and wait for her to come home. When she was gone on weekends, I missed my mom the most because everyone else had their parents at home with them. And for the most part, they usually spent time with their children, so I was not able to play with my cousins, and there was no school to help keep me occupied either. Mom usually showed up somewhere around 4:00 p.m. As soon as I saw her getting out of the tricycle, a motorcycle with a side car, I would run down the stairs so fast saying, "Mama's home, mama's home!" I think at times I would get too loud because my aunt had to ask me to lower my voice often. My mom wasn't affectionate and didn't really like showing any kind of emotion. When my sister and I would kiss her on the cheek, she would make a facial expression that looked like we had a beard or something. I asked her once why she would do that. She said she wasn't used to it so that made her feel weird. We still kissed her anyway and simply ignored her response. On the other hand, my dad was very affectionate and gracious and full of compliments when he liked you.

It was all conditional, of course. When my mom arrived home, she would go directly to my grandma's bedroom and stay there for a bit while they took time to discuss her life. Most often, my grandma lectured my mom. She usually lectured my mom about her responsibilities to me. I don't really know how my mom would respond because I could barely hear her. When they got done talking, my mom would grab a pillow and read her favorite book. She usually read Barbara Cartland or Harold Robbins books. I followed my mom around the house like a puppy, anywhere she went. She would lie down on the wood floor and start reading. I sat right above her head while she read. I can't remember exactly what I would do while sitting there, but I do remember not playing or going anywhere because I wanted to be near her so badly. I missed her so much when she wasn't home.

Around 9:00 p.m. my mom would ask the house help to purchase a pint of rum for her. She would mix it with Coca-Cola and drink it slowly, and then when she got too tired, she would go to bed. I remember hugging her when we slept. There were times when her cousins and only brother would drink with her. I followed them around too. I would sit quietly beside my mom while they drank. They usually had finger foods to go with the liquor. They would tell jokes that would make all of us roll on the floor in laughter. In fact, their jokes were so funny I can still remember some of them today. Sometimes they told stories about the trouble they would get into because they were so drunk—their passing out or knocking on someone else's door mistakenly in a drunken stupor were sure favorites.

At times we laughed so hard that my aunt had to come downstairs to ask everyone to please be more considerate and keep the noise down. She was the eldest, and everyone referred to her as "corny" or a killjoy. Even though they would all acquiesce, as soon as she turned her back they would all burst into laughter. Obviously, they behaved just like little children.

I have to admit that I, too, thought it was hilarious. But after only a few months, my mom started coming home less and less. Even so, I still sat by the window every Friday afternoon hoping my mom would show up that evening. There was a time when I thought I saw her getting out of the tricycle, but it was nothing but my hopeful imagination. I think I was so desperate for her to come home that I actually ended up hallucinating.

Finally, when I couldn't wait any longer, I decided I was going to skip class to look for my mom. I really didn't know how to take public transportation because I was young and my dad and my aunt had a car. I knew how to take the jeepneys and tricycle but only for a five-mile distance at the most because this was the way I went to church or to the public market. It had been months since I last saw my mom. Something inside me was overwhelmed with worry. I couldn't help but think, What if she was run over by a car because she was drunk? All of a sudden, the stories they used to talk about didn't seem to be nearly as funny anymore.

That day, I took all my schoolbooks out of my bag and replaced them with a change of clothes. I wore a uniform to school, and I couldn't walk outside the campus wearing it. I saved up a few bucks, enough to take the public transportation. I wasn't really sure that it was enough money, but I truthfully didn't care. The school bus came in the morning to pick me up, and then when we got dropped off on the campus, I went to the girls' restroom right away and changed very quickly. I tried to fold my uniform carefully to avoid having it get so wrinkled that my grandma might notice. I came out of the restroom transformed, wearing a summer dress, flat shoes, and sunglasses. When I passed the school guard, he didn't even know who I was!

I wasn't really sure why I felt so free when I got off the campus. I hailed a jeepney, and the driver stopped. "How do I get to the Malate church, sir?" I inquired politely. He said he was going that way, and it was only two pesos and fifty cents to get there.

Then he told me he would stop right in front of the church. So I took that jeepney and was on it for about an hour and a half. I realized my mom wasn't lying to my grandma when she said it was too much hassle to come home. I honestly wasn't scared at all, just anxiously wondering if I would be able to find my mom. I was also worried that I needed to get back to school in time for my school bus or my grandma would find out. "Here we are, kid, the Malate church," the driver said. I told him thank you and stepped down from the jeepney.

The church was so beautiful inside. It had all the saints and was so quiet. I liked the peace! When I came out, I surveyed the streets.

There were houses on both the left and right side of the street. I kept thinking my mom had mentioned that it was right beside the Malate church so I figured it shouldn't be too far from where I was at the church. I decided I was going to walk down the streets yelling for her. I reasoned that if she would hear my voice, she would definitely come out. This was fairly early in the morning because I went to school at 7:00 a.m.

So I started to walk on the right side of the street first and yelled, "Ma! Ma!" I passed about five houses until someone from above yelled, "Hey, what are you doing here, and how did you find me?" She told me to wait there because she was coming down. I was so excited. When she opened the door, I saw a narrow hallway with a very steep stairway. My mom invited me to come up. She was wearing a pink-colored negligee. It wasn't see-through or anything but just flowed like silk while she climbed the stairs. When we got to the top, it revealed a tiny living room. She asked me to be quiet because her neighbors were in the other room. Evidently, they shared the living room, kitchen, and bathroom, sort of like a communal home. Once we walked inside her room, I was astounded to see a man lying there on the bed in his underwear. I had no idea she lived with a gentleman. She had told my grandma her roommate was a woman. I kept silent and didn't say a word.

Mom knew I was shocked, but she acted like it was no big deal. She asked me once more how I found out where she lived; then she asked if I was hungry. She fed me breakfast, and then I told her that grandma didn't know I had come to see her. I didn't get in trouble for my visit to her house that day. I wasn't there that long; I had to leave because I didn't want my grandma to know that I left school without permission. I got back to school the same way I came, only this time I asked the driver what bus I had to take to get to Marikina, the town where my school was. I think I was fortunate to get back to school in time to take the school bus home. And when I got home, I never talked

about my trip to see my mom. My mom never really asked me to lie,
but I knew that I wasn't supposed to say anything to protect her.

That night I couldn't help but cry myself to sleep because I fully
realized that my mom and dad were never going to get back together
again. This revelation truly broke my heart. The one good thing that
came out of that day was that my sister and I were then allowed to go
visit my mom. We were able to see her almost every weekend. When
we went to see her, my mom would prepare our favorite foods such as
crabs, fried chicken, and prawns. Both my sister and I would eat to
our heart's content. Then my dad's driver would take us back home.
Those were fun memories for me because I was with the two people I
loved the most, my sister and my mom.

During this time, we also met my mom's neighbors. They were
a husband, a wife, and a brother-in-law. The brother-in-law was very
fond of me, so whenever I came to visit, he would make a big stack
of pancakes. I am not too sure how he found out I loved them, but
I didn't really care. I just ate them when he gave them to me. This
man was in his 40s. One day I cut class again to visit my mom. She
wasn't there though, but he was. He started some small talk and then
asked if I wanted to come see his new car. I wasn't really interested,
but I was being polite for all the "dang" pancakes he was giving me,
so I said okay.

We went downstairs where the car was parked in front of my
mom's window. It was a red sports car and was kind of nice. He asked
me if I would like to see the interior of his car, and I said okay. Then
he opened the door for me, and as he did, he stuck a gun into my side
and ordered me to get in. At first I was completely confused, and I got
into the car without any fuss. I sat there while he got into the driver's
seat. As we drove off, he started talking about how much he liked me
and told me that I shouldn't be afraid of him because he planned on
marrying me at his mosque. As a matter of fact, he again stated that
was exactly where we were headed.

I stayed quiet and didn't say a word while he drove. For some strange reason, I was calm. I think I was caught by such surprise that I was actually in shock and didn't understand what was happening. However, after a while I started to assess the situation and realized the best thing for me to do was to keep very calm and act like I wouldn't mind being married to him. We drove to Quiapo, which was the town where the Muslim mosque was located. He parked and put his gun away. He went to the car door and opened it for me. When we got to the mosque, he realized it was closed. I could tell he was very disappointed. He spoke to a man in their native dialect, which I didn't understand because I only spoke Tagalog.

Then he turned to me and explained the mosque would not be open until tomorrow morning so we would get married then. I casually said it was okay. After that we got back inside his car and proceeded to his mother's home. When we arrived, I found everyone was speaking in his own dialect. I was very scared because there were so many of them and I couldn't understand one word of what they were talking about. I was really afraid that they were going to take me to the Mindanao Islands because that is where they were originally from. Women have no rights there, and they are Muslims. They kept looking at me repeatedly while they were talking. I tried very hard to act calm and collected. At one point I even grabbed a magazine and pretended to read it because I didn't know how to keep myself composed.

They had prepared food, and everyone started to eat. Their food was very different from our food in Manila. This made me very leery to eat anything, but they kept insisting I eat so I sampled some of the dishes that looked okay. My stomach wasn't feeling very well; I wanted to throw up but somehow managed to hold it together. I didn't want to show any sign of fear, and I felt it would be safest for me if he continued to believe that this whole thing was not against my will. After dinner he started to say goodbye to everyone. He told me we were leaving and that we would be able to see them all again the next day at our wedding around noon. He brought three of his cousins along, and they rode with us.

At this point, I didn't know where we were headed, and the dark sky seemed only to escalate my fears. I was thankful it was too dark for him to see my face. I was too alert studying my surroundings in the event an opportunity to run away presented itself. But I knew there was no way I would ever be able to get away from him. It felt like we drove for a long time before he came to a stop in front of a hotel. I could literally feel my stomach start to turn. I might have been only 13 years old, but I certainly knew what people did in hotels. He checked us in, and then we walked up to the room. When we got there, he ordered some beer and asked me if I would like some. I told him, no thank you.

After he finished about three bottles of beer, he came over to me, took my clothes off, and had sex with me. I didn't try to fight him and did exactly what he asked of me. I lay there in pain, but I didn't cry. I was thinking about how disgusting and repulsive it was to me to have this man on top of me. His breath stunk like beer. I found myself wondering how long this was supposed to last and was questioning whether he was going to do this to me over and over again. All of a sudden, he stopped. There was no conversation between us, and not one word was spoken the entire time. He just rolled over and fell asleep.

When I heard him snoring, my heart started pounding as I got up very slowly. I tried to clean myself up without throwing up. I got dressed and carefully tiptoed around the room. I was so afraid that I was going to wake him up. When I got to the door to open it, I thought maybe I should peek through the little window to make sure it was safe outside. To my utter dismay, the men who rode with us were standing by the door guarding it. I went to the bathroom and put a towel over my mouth so I could hyperventilate without waking him up. I was so terrified! I went back to lie down beside this man with my clothes on because I didn't want him to think I tried to get away. I figured

I would find an opportunity to escape sometime in the morning. Because I couldn't sleep, I stayed awake all night thinking, Please don't let him do this to me again when he wakes up. When he woke up that morning he went straight to the restroom to get ready. I was so relieved.

When I got ready, I tried to wash away what happened to me the night before, but there was no amount of scrubbing that seemed like enough to ever take it away. When we came out of the room, the men who were standing guard the night before were gone. He checked us out and we drove to Cubao, a town much like Pasadena in California. After a while, I broke my silence and said to him, "Isn't our wedding at noon? Why don't we go see a movie first?" He smiled a little bit and said that would be okay. So we drove to where the theaters were. All this time I was trying to survey every place we drove and was thinking about how I could possibly get away from him. Then we came to the Alta theaters; right across the highway was a huge Mercury Drug store with glass doors. I decided this was my opportunity to escape.

I asked him to please go to the drugstore because I couldn't walk anymore. I explained that the blister from my new shoes was so big and it had filled with water. I even took off my shoes to show him. The funny thing was that I really did have a blister, but I never really felt the pain until that moment when I actually looked at it closely. He looked at my big blister, and I could tell that he felt bad for me. He agreed to go to the drugstore for me, and I told him I would stay in the car and wait. I watched him cross the street. It took him awhile because he had to watch carefully and make sure there weren't any cars coming before he crossed the busy street. He finally got across, and I was watching him very closely through the glass windows.

As soon as he started talking to the sales lady, I quickly ran away from his car and went right out on the road to hail any car that would stop for me. I was crying while doing this, and a red truck pulled up. I got in and there were no other passengers inside but myself. At this point, I was hysterical, and I asked the man to please drive fast and try to lose the guy who was frantically getting into his car to follow us. The man in the red truck did exactly what I asked. He drove so fast that we lost my predator after a few miles or so. When the driver of the red truck realized I was safe, he asked me where he should take me. I realized I couldn't go back to my mom's place where the man lived. Then I remembered befriending an older woman who had eight children some time before, so I asked the driver to take me there. He dropped me off, and then he was gone. I never even knew his name. To this day, I sincerely believe God sent an angel to rescue me.

So you see, to come back to the Malate church to seek refuge was nothing new to me. This particular night, after leaving my mom's house for good, I got there on time for the 6:00 p.m. service and attended the mass. I asked God, "What am I supposed to do? Where do I go from here?" The mass was in progress, but I really had no idea what was being said or how it related to my situation. That had always been my experience going to church. I did it because I was raised to attend it, loved the choir, enjoyed the lyrics of the songs, and felt safe inside. I have always known and believed that there is a God, but to me, He was this big guy up there whom I couldn't reach.

Frankly speaking, I felt like He was just waiting for me to mess up so He could reach down and punish me. When the mass was over, they started to clean up inside the church. I felt my fear overpower me when it came back because I really didn't know what to do. "Excuse me, you have to leave now because we have to lock up the church," a man said to me. I took my bag and stood right by the door of the church as he shut the door behind me. The church was located on a busy street across from Shakey's Pizza and a few nightclubs. I walked over to my mom's old apartment just to look at it again. It was quiet and appeared to be empty. It brought back memories of that day when I located my mom for the first time.

Then I turned around toward the church and decided to sit on the bench by the church grounds. While I sat there, I watched people come and go. A few couples walked by hand-in-hand on their dates, and I recall observing a few families as they passed. The lights on the streets were bright, so I wasn't really frightened until later when the people who walked by started to become few and far between. I looked at the clock; it read 11:00 p.m. By midnight, several drunken people, mostly men, started coming out of the bars and Shakey's Pizza. I decided I should move to a different location because the "crazies" were suddenly approaching me.

Malate church was more likely a small cathedral, so to speak. I surveyed the grounds, realizing that the other side of it was facing the church's kitchen and there was a very dark but hidden alley. I decided this was the safest place for me to spend the night, so there I sat by the door of the church, using my bag as my pillow. I figured that because this was God's house, nothing could harm me. It seemed to me that God would protect me once again. When morning came, the church's caretaker saw me curled up in the alley. She took pity on me immediately and told me to wait by the door. When she came back, she brought me the priests' leftover food from the dining room.

The church housed six priests who came from different parts of the world. One of them, Father Benjamin, was from the United States. One afternoon, he called out to me and asked me why I was staying on the church grounds. I began to tell him what had happened to me, and I realized it made me feel better. It was probably because I was used to confessing my sins inside the confessional, except this one was a treat! I was doing my confession with the priest in person; we were literally face-to-face.

Father Benjamin was very nice and gracious to me. He suggested that I go back home because it was extremely dangerous for me to be living outside the church on the streets. By now I had been staying there for three days with no shower. I did follow his advice, but not exactly. I went to the house of my Indian friends whom I met at church when I used to come see my mom. This family had three sisters who were in their early 20s. The middle sister liked me so much that she suggested I could stay with them. The only stipulation was that if their mother came to their room, I would have to hide.

During this time, their father was very ill, which took an extreme amount of their mother's time and energy. She was a devout Christian. Fortunately, I didn't have to hide very often so this worked out all right. Father Benjamin gave me a part-time job at the church that I thoroughly enjoyed. I took over when the church secretary was not available. I scheduled baptisms, weddings, and whatever it was that people wanted to do at the church. Whenever I was there, I met with Father Benjamin, and we would discuss my life. I am so thankful that my dad sent my sister and me to a great private school because English was a second language to me. Obviously, this made it possible for us to communicate. My friends didn't speak very much Tagalog either. They smoked and drank occasionally, so at age 15 going on 16, I was already smoking. I didn't drink though. I was afraid of alcohol because of what I had seen it do to my mom's life; therefore, I made a vow to myself never to be a drunk. I stayed with these Indian friends for three years off and on, struggling to continue schooling. I moved around so much during this time of my life, and it was the loneliest period of my existence.

Chapter Ten

Working Out My Faith

I seriously felt like ever since I stepped foot into the United States, all I had done was move around repeatedly. The truth was that I was willing to do whatever it took to get us here, but when push came to shove, I wasn't actually willing to risk my daughter's life. At the same time, not everyone gets an opportunity to live in the United States legally while awaiting a pending petition. That day when Forman pointed out to me through the window where the INS cars were located, I calmed down. Seeing them parked right across from my house made me feel safer.

The next day, I went to work, and Maryl went to school on our usual schedule. I asked one of my good friends at work to help me find a new place to live as soon as possible. After just a week, she found a back room for me to rent. It was in the San Fernando Valley on Magnolia Street, and I was very excited to see it. My friend and I went to see the place, and we were able to meet with the owner. The moment we drove onto the street, it felt familiar, like home to me because it was in a very quiet and clean neighborhood. Big trees lined the streets, and the houses were fairly good-sized as well. When we knocked on the door, an older man appeared, probably in his late 70s or early 80s. He was very pleasant, and he motioned for us to go through the side wood gate, which led to the alley side of the house. He opened a bedroom door that was attached to the house. Apparently it was at one time a garage that had been converted into a bedroom. Inside the room was a small sink, a tiny walk-in closet, a good-sized full bath, and a sliding glass door that overlooked a very small yard. The glass sliding door created a feeling of openness, and it did not feel claustrophobic. I loved it so much I promptly asked him how much the rent was and what the requirements were for the renter. I told him about my little girl, and he said that would be okay. He then informed me that he required the first and last month's deposit.

I had the money with me so I paid him right on the spot. When I picked up Maryl after school, I told her the good news. She was really excited too, and I told her we were moving in only two days. As usual, it didn't take us very long to gather up all our things to move. At this point, our belongings only consisted of a queen-sized bed, a blue recliner, a 27-inch television, a video player, a radio, a few plates, two pots and pans, and our clothes. Maryl and I were so happy that we finally had a place that felt like home. The location felt safe because no one could see us unless they went to the back of the house. It was very private and hidden. Our landlord and his wife were a nice Jewish couple. They didn't have any children, and just the two of them lived in the house. In the mornings they had a Filipina caregiver who came to care for the wife, who had recently had brain cancer surgery.

We finally felt settled, at long last! Maryl especially loved our landlord, and she lovingly called him Grandpa. He used to babysit her for free. He would bring a cooked meal to us quite often. While we lived there, we adopted a stray cat that Maryl named Lily. I didn't mind having her at all because Lily woke Maryl every day before school. Finally, my days of having to drag her out of bed and push her to shower were gone. Now, all I had to do was put Lily on the bed, and she would do the waking. Lily would lick Maryl's face, and I would tell her that the cat wanted her to get up. Then she would wake up just like that! I bought us a single electric stove, which I set up outside. I cooked Filipino food because it was cheaper for us, and Maryl liked it. When it rained, I used an umbrella to cook outside. I remember one of Maryl's drawings in school depicted me holding an umbrella while I was cooking in the rain. I liked it so much that I framed this valued picture.

I continued working for the marketing research company in Los Angeles. The INS called for me to assist them less and less. I did a few cases for them that took me to Las Vegas at times, but none of these cases was ever as big as the Mabuhay case. The first Sunday we lived in our new home, Maryl and I went to the church on Colorado Blvd. for the last time. I usually sat on the very front row because I didn't like getting distracted. On that day, however, I purposefully sat at the very back row. I knelt down, staring at the crucifix as I started to talk to God. "God, I know that You are there, but I don't know if You are there for me. At times I think maybe You are not, because if You were there, then why has my life been nothing but pain. Why is it that when I come to church, I don't feel any different? I feel the same way I came in. Wasn't I supposed to feel good or something? I am going to have to say goodbye to You now. I will never come back to this church again or to any church for that matter. And if I am wrong and You do exist, then You will find me and bring me back to You. But until then, this is it for us."

I walked out of that church with a very heavy heart. I didn't feel any guilt for the first time in my life. But it made me feel like I had just let go of a relationship. It felt like I was grieving. I didn't tell Maryl about my decision. I think a part of me was hoping that God would find me and bring me back to Him, because I had never lived my life without Him.

For the next two years after that vow in the back row of the church, I lived my life without giving God a thought or permitting myself to do so. I got involved in astrology, and I was worshiping nature. I led a God-free life, so to speak. It was also during this time that I started to feel "Americanized," as I called it. I felt well adjusted. My Filipino accent was not as obvious as it used to be. I had become popular at my job and developed great friendships. My best friends were one of the male project directors and the female assistant in the accounting department. The three of us had become inseparable. I started to party with them. I loved dancing! I would have a drink but still never allowed myself to get to the point of oblivion and losing control. When I started to feel tipsy, I would very quickly stop because I was afraid to become an alcoholic. I knew I was predisposed looking at my family history. I had set some boundaries when it came to partying. My friends knew I didn't particularly like going out during the weekends because those belonged to Maryl. Occasionally I would go out on a Saturday, but it was never that often. It was usually on a Friday.

One Friday night my friends and I were in a club somewhere

on Ventura Blvd. in California. I distinctly remember a slow song playing as I worked my way up to the bar to get a drink for myself. I ordered a blended margarita. While I was talking to the bartender, a very good-looking man across the other side of the bar kept smiling at me. I tried to ignore him because I hated men during that time of my life. I had no respect for them. I thought they were only after one thing, that is, using a woman for sexual pleasure and nothing else. As a matter of fact, on those very few occasions that I would go out on a date, I would manage to turn him off by the second date. I was very blatant regarding this matter: "I know how this works. You will take me to dinner at least twice and then expect me to go to bed with you by the third date. Well, I will not sleep with you, so you may want to rethink that second date." And that would do it. The strange thing about this whole situation was that it still hurt my feelings even if I had expected it.

It made me hate men all the more because it confirmed my view of them each time it happened. I completely ignored this man across the other side of the bar. But I have to admit, I was very attracted to him because he was very good-looking—tall, lean, and blonde with blue eyes! I walked back to my friends' table and sat down. It hadn't been 15 minutes when the same man approached me. He looked at my friends to apologize for his intrusion but then turned to me to say, "My name is John. I saw you at the bar, and I have to say you are one of the prettiest women I have ever seen!" He started to hand his driver's license to me and continued on to explain that he was not a bad person, that he was a good, law-abiding citizen! To that I was dumbfounded because I had never heard that one before. *What a line!* I thought. My friends were watching the whole time, encouraging me to give this guy an opportunity. So I did. I gave him my work phone number. One week after, we met for dinner. I asked to meet him at the restaurant because another dating rule of mine was to "bring my own car." This would guarantee that I was not trapped in his car just in case it was a bad experience or he happened to be an ax murderer.

John turned out to be a very nice person. We had been spending time together for a little bit when during one of our dinners together, he asked if I went to church. I wasn't sure what to answer because my goal was "to give the answer he wants to hear." We hadn't passed the "impress me" stage of dating. Instead of answering his question, I evaded by asking him, "Do you?" Matter-of-factly he said, "I do!" He continued to say that he and his mother go to one of the churches in the Valley. He asked if I would like to go with him and his mother that following Sunday. Without any hesitation, I said, "Sure!" All the while I was thinking to myself that this was a good sign, introducing me to his mother. *It was a big deal, and he must really like me,* I thought. I wasn't interested in going to church, but I sure was interested in John. He gave me the address to the church, and at exactly 9:00 a.m. on that Sunday, I met him and his mother at the church grounds. For the first time I introduced them to Maryl. I could tell they were both taken aback, as I had never mentioned Maryl to John. It was my way of protecting her. Maryl was very polite and pleased to meet them. She liked them both instantaneously. When they asked if she wanted to go to Sunday school, I was surprised that she agreed so quickly. After we dropped her off, we proceeded to the main sanctuary. When we started to approach the place, I was astounded to hear loud music playing and people singing.

I was shaken by the sight of people's hands raised up in the air as they sang! Some had their eyes shut, and some were kneeling with their hands up in the air. Some of these people were dressed in shorts, some in jeans, and others were wearing dresses. I tried not to look so appalled, but I was. Being born and raised Catholic, this was very unfamiliar; we conducted church in orderliness and wore formal outfits. I could tell John's mother noticed how uncomfortable I was. All I wanted to do was run out of there. I thought, *Oh my God, these people are absolutely out of their minds!* But I stayed because I didn't want them to be offended. When all the singing and what seemed to me to be chaos ended, the pastor came up to the pulpit, greeted everybody, and started to talk. I can't remember specifically what he talked about, but I do remember he was very personable and put me at ease. When it was over, we picked up Maryl, said our good-byes, and went our own separate ways. I tried not to think about the experience that day, but Maryl sure had fun. She said she wouldn't mind going back because the children were nice to her.

I didn't hear from John for the next few days. In fact, a few weeks went by and still no phone call at all. I started to wonder why and became very tempted to call him, but my grandmother once told me, "Never pursue the man; let him pursue you!" so I didn't call. Instead, I planned to go back on the next Sunday to that church because I knew John and his mother would be there. Besides, Maryl liked it.

The following Sunday, we went back to that church again. As I parked our car, I saw John's mother walking toward us with a smile on her face and a big kiss for Maryl. I didn't ask her where John was, but I really wanted to. When we walked in, the music hadn't started, but I could feel a knot in my stomach. I was already feeling anxious. We sat beside each other for about 10 minutes, and then the band started to sing. She got up, so I got up. And a beautiful song filled the entire room, *"Amazing grace, how sweet the sound that saved a wretch like me, I once was lost but now am found, was blind but now I see."* The lyrics of the song were plastered on the huge screen overhead, and I couldn't help but focus on those words. I started to cry, so close to sobbing. I was confused and couldn't understand why I was reacting to the song in this way, not to mention the embarrassment I was feeling with John's mother right beside me. I kept thinking to myself, *Stop crying; what's wrong with you?* But those words "a wretch like me" reverberated in my head. Wasn't that what I had been feeling all my life? After the rejection from my parents and my family, being kidnapped and then raped, the relationship with Maryl's biological father, and having a child out of wedlock, those words described exactly what I felt I was.

From the outside, I looked all right and well put together, but not inside. John's mother then turned to me with a gentle smile on her face and whispered, "It's okay, sweetheart; it's the Holy Spirit touching you." Well, that confused me even more because I had no idea what she meant. I was feeling some sort of soothing inside of me, something I had never felt before, and it was quite unfamiliar. When the song ended, I sat down and tried to pull myself together. The pastor came up to the pulpit just like the previous time; I found myself listening to him, paying extra attention to what he had to say. He started to talk about salvation—a word that I had never heard before. He also talked about having a personal relationship with Jesus Christ. He said, "If you confess with your mouth the Lord Jesus and believe in your heart that God has raised Him from the dead, you will be saved." He made it sound so easy. I was thinking to myself, *That's all I needed to do? What about my penance? Wasn't there anything I needed to do to show or prove my repentance?*

Then, as if the pastor were reading my mind, he asked if there was anyone in the room who would like to accept the invitation of receiving Jesus Christ as their Lord and Savior. I started to feel uneasy and apprehensive even more. My heart started beating fast, and my hands became sweaty. I was thinking, *I do! I do!* But I felt too embarrassed to walk up in front of all the people. Before I could even finish that thought, however, John's mother turned to me to say, "Would you like to go up there? I can walk with you." Tears started streaming down my face as I accepted her offer. As I worked my way to the pulpit where the pastor was, my knees felt frail. I tried not to look at anyone in that room. Much to my surprise, I was not the only person who was going up there. Although the walk seemed like an eternity, I kept going.

When all of us got there, the pastor asked the church congregation to join him in prayer. Everyone in that room shut their eyes with smiles on their faces. It was a very simple and short prayer, but it meant the world to me. I barely remember the exact words he uttered, but I do remember him thanking God for those of us who were up there and that we had chosen to allow God into our lives. He also said to us that if we confess our sins and turn from them, God forgives and removes all our sins and we become as white as snow. I started to cry again, but this time they were tears of joy. For the first time in a very long time, I felt free. It felt like a heavy weight was lifted off my shoulders. It was the year 1993 when I accepted God back into my life, and two weeks after, Maryl and I were baptized together.

Later on I found out that John was struggling for his sobriety. We continued to go to the church in the Valley with his mother, without John. I found out that the church provided free showers for the homeless once a month. I figured it would be a good idea for Maryl and me to help out. Because I knew how to cut hair, I provided free haircuts for the homeless while they waited for their turn to shower, and Maryl read to the little children who came with their parents; they too received a free haircut.

After a few months, I finally heard from John; he was sober. He apologized for not telling me the truth and confessed how much he hated the alcoholism that plagued him. "I just can't kick it," he said. He told me that his mother and father were both alcoholics when he was conceived, and that both his parents got sober when he was about 7 years old, the same year they became Christians. He professed his love for God and how much he hated himself for continuously disappointing God and his parents. He asked me for another chance and promised me that this time, he would stay sober and clean for good. I remember feeling empathy for him; I didn't want him to feel like I had no faith in him. In my heart I wanted him to win and conquer alcoholism. *After all,* I thought, *he has God in his heart and He certainly would help him get healed.*

So I was on a mission, and I decided I would do everything I could in my power to help John get sober. I even allowed him to babysit Maryl once in a while even after I got a call from his mother warning me that it wasn't a good idea. "He will not physically hurt her, I know that, but he can get drunk and not remember where he left her!" she said. Maryl loved John, and he loved her. He was very sweet and gentle to her; as a matter of fact, whenever Maryl got in trouble with me, John would be so angry with me, which of course irritated me. *What does he know about parenting,* I thought.

Early in the morning one day, around 2:00 a.m., a very loud banging on the sliding door of our bedroom startled Maryl and me. I jumped out of bed frightened; I quietly motioned for Maryl to stay down and not move. As I peeked through the blinds to see who it was, I was astounded to see John standing in front of the glass door. His face was covered with blood, and his eyes, although gazing straight at me, seemed like he was looking through me; they were red and dilated. I didn't open the door; instead, I yelled for him to get out of our yard or I would call the cops. I could tell he didn't like that very much because he started to press himself against the sliding door and banged on it all the more. He started swearing, threatening, and saying I was out of my mind. I didn't waste another minute, immediately dialing 911.

In a matter of 15 minutes, police officers were at our home. As soon as they got there, John tried to stand still and straightened up, working very hard at looking sober. The officers stood right beside him and started to talk to him as though he were a little boy. As I paid attention to what was going on, I realized the police officers knew John was completely out of his head. I kept looking back at Maryl trying to make sure she didn't come out and see what was going on. But I knew it was too late; Maryl did see John's bloody face. After what seemed like an eternity, the officers came up to me to ask if I would like to press charges. That thought didn't even cross my mind. Although I was very angry, I certainly didn't want to see John in jail because deep inside I felt very sorry for him. The officers said okay and assured me that John would not be coming back or they would take him straight to jail.

When they left, I asked Maryl if she was okay. I hugged her and apologized for what she had just witnessed. I put her back to bed, and she went right back to sleep. But I didn't. I sat there thinking what a horrible mother I was, subjecting my child to what had just happened. I thought how I was re-creating my life all over again and how I felt I had ruined Maryl. That night, I made a definite decision never to speak to John again. A few weeks after that incident, John tried to call me at work—at times sober, other times so drunk I couldn't even make out the words that were coming out of his mouth. A part of me wanted to be friendly and kind, but instead I would just hang up the phone. I decided, however, not to end the friendship Maryl and I shared with John's mother. We continued to go to church with her every Sunday and go to breakfast after the church service. She would voluntarily tell me John's whereabouts, which I didn't mind at all. In a lot of ways, I was very proud of her; I admired her for not allowing John's disease to take over her life. She taught me a lot about the disease of alcoholism. I learned about myself, about my mom, and about how much my mom's own alcoholism affected me. I realized I was a caretaker, because I took care of my mom for the most part of my childhood. This revelation caused me to experience very deep sadness. I started to examine my life.

I knew that going to church was starting to affect me in a lot of ways. I started to have hope again, and I was talking to God and praying again. I even told God one day that I was very tired of trying to look for a good father for Maryl. I prayed, *"I only pick sick losers, Lord, so from here on, I am going to stop searching. You pick the man for me."* But I thought I should give God the specifics just in case He decided to give him to me. So I took out a yellow pad and started to write down the characteristics in a man that I was looking for. Number 1 on my list was that he must love God above all. Number 2, he must not be a child molester; 3, he must be a good father to Maryl; 4, he must not be an alcoholic; 5, he must be willing to marry; and so on. Needless to say, the list went on and on; it got up to number 70. I even asked God for a man who was blonde with blue eyes and not shorter than 6 feet. When I got done with the list, I folded it once and stuck it in my Bible. There it rested, as I believed with all of my heart that God would find this man for me.

For the first time in my life I wasn't scared to be a single mother. I completely gave up on the idea that I needed to marry a financially stable man to help me raise Maryl. I found a new sense of security. I tried to calculate how old I would be when Maryl would finally go away to college. I figured I would be in my 40s, which is really not that old to start a relationship with someone, and it would be perfect. In retrospect, the way I was thinking was a lot more pleasant. Of course I continued to spend time with my friends. There were six of us in the group; four of them were Jewish, and the other two I didn't really know where they stood in religious matters. Not one of them ever made me feel judged or rejected. They respected my newfound way of life and were happy for me. I respected their beliefs and preferences as well, so whenever we got together, it was never an issue.

The more I attended church, the more I started thinking about how I was leading my life. The pastor at our church never really said we would go to hell if we drank, cursed, smoked, and so on. Most of his teachings were about "giving God a try" instead of relying on our own strength. I liked that he taught from the Bible and didn't divert from it. He never made me feel condemned or bad about myself. Something inside of me was changing, however. Although I was never a drunk, I smoked two packs of Marlboro Reds per day, depending on my stress level. I cursed all the time; as a matter of fact, I used the "F" word as a verb and adjective. I was also a control freak. I didn't trust anyone to do a job better than I could. I cleaned all the time, yet I was not really sure why. I would get home from work late in the evening and still find the energy to clean. I was high-strung and often restless, and I worried myself sick about everything. I felt like everything depended on me. I was afraid to trust anyone. I didn't really like women, except for my group of friends. I didn't actually like people in general. I used to think that people were nice to me because they needed something or wanted something. It was very difficult for me to believe that someone would actually like me for who I was without a hidden agenda. I was in "defense" mode 24/7, so it's no wonder I was always exhausted. It was too much of a burden to carry.

People I worked with didn't really like me. They were scared of me because I had no problem telling them how I felt when they didn't do their job. I didn't just get angry; I would literally go into rage. To this day, I cannot forget how badly I treated Marie, one of the girls I worked with. Each morning she would come to work and the first thing that came out of her mouth was, "I don't want to be here; I hate this place!" The comment bothered me so much but I never said a word—until one day, when I missed a deadline because she failed to do her part of the job. I stormed downstairs fuming, looking for Marie. I found her laughing while she was telling the story of her partying the night before. As you can imagine, this just pushed me to the edge as I yelled, "Marie! This is the reason nothing here gets done. You're lazy and useless! Why don't you do us all a favor and quit! You hate this place anyway!" I believed everyone around stood there in disbelief. As I walked back to my office, I felt this overwhelming feeling of guilt and remorse. The incident bothered me all day.

When I got home that night, I prayed and asked God to forgive me for treating Marie so badly. The very next morning, I searched for Marie to apologize. I knew where to find her, outside with her cup of coffee and cigarettes. When she saw me coming, her face looked scared, and as I got closer, she seemed frozen. I said, "Marie, I wanted to tell you how sorry I am for all of the things that I said to you yesterday. I wish I could take them back, but I can't. And if you choose not to forgive me, I understand. But I still want you to know, you did not deserve to be treated that way. I am really very sorry." My eyes filled with tears. I think Marie was taken aback because it was not like me to apologize. The only people I apologized to were Maryl and the people who could influence my paycheck. But one of the things I started to learn at church was forgiveness. I couldn't rationalize my rage and bad behavior anymore. The night before, I kept thinking that I didn't have the right to treat people the way I did. *If God has forgiven me, who am I not to forgive? And who was I to treat Marie that way?* I believed that God loved me as much as He loved Marie.

The change in me was gradual and at times very slow. My faith was very emotional; when I was up, my faith was strong, but when things didn't go the way I wanted them to, my faith "tanked" because I would automatically think God was mad at me. I never doubted that He loved me; I just doubted that He would not punish me.

At one point I came so very close to giving up on my new-found faith. I had just gotten paid the night before, and that next morning I went to attend my step class at the gym. I had $500 in my wallet because I intended to pay the rent when I got home. When the step class ended, I quickly dashed out of there only to realize halfway to the parking lot that I had left my wallet on the floor of the classroom. I turned around so fast to get to my wallet before anyone could, hoping against hope that it would still be there, but I knew my efforts were futile. I had a feeling of resignation as I walked out of there without my wallet. I couldn't understand why God would allow this to happen. *Doesn't He know I had no other way to get money until the next paycheck?* And although my landlord was a good man, he needed the rent paid on time. To top that off, a week after that incident, Maryl and I got into a car accident and I totaled my car. This meant no money, no way to get to work, and no way to get Maryl to school. *Well, that does it!* I thought. In a friend's car, I drove to our church in Reseda, and I demanded to see the pastor. When he came out, I literally attacked him, as if it were his fault that all of these things were happening to me. "You know what? When I wasn't a Christian, my life was hard but not this hard. How can God do this to me? I am done with this church thing! I will never come here again, ever!"

Much to my surprise, the pastor was very calm and genuinely empathized with me. I was waiting for him to say to me, "How dare you," but he didn't. Instead, he said that he could understand my distress and that he was sorry for what had happened. I was left not knowing what to say in response to his statement; I wasn't used to the kind gesture. I started to walk away, but before I could, he said, "Will you wait here for just a minute? I wanted to give you something before you leave." It wasn't more than five minutes when he came back with a white letter envelope in his hands. He handed it to me and said, "Here is $500. The Lord wanted me to give it to you so you can pay your house rent. You don't have to pay it back. If someday you are in the position to, sure; otherwise, please consider this a gift from God." I was speechless for a few seconds, and then I said, "No way. I am not taking this money. What if I can't pay it back? I don't want to be punished!" The pastor patiently smiled and said, "You are not required to pay it back; please take it." I was hesitant but only for another minute, and then I left. I don't think I even said thank you. During the drive home, I felt a twinge of guilt, but I ignored it. Deep inside I thought, God owed it to me.

When I got home I handed the money to my landlord. I ended up borrowing $200 from one of the project directors in our company, who also happened to be a very good friend and neighbor of mine. She also offered Maryl and me a ride to get to where we needed to go for as long as we needed it. She refused to take gas money from me or any form of cash payment.

It wasn't very long until I was able to buy a secondhand car that had 70,000 miles on it, but it worked great and the price was right. Long story short, I was back to my normal schedule. I tried to stay away from the church but not for long. When Maryl asked why we had not gone, I lied by telling her I was not feeling good. The truth was, it felt like something was missing in my life when we didn't go to church, but I was very embarrassed with the way I behaved toward the pastor. After missing two Sundays of church,

I finally got the courage to go back. When the pastor saw me, he acted like nothing had transpired between us. He even came up to me for a nice gentle hug and said, "I am so glad you're here today." I smiled, and deep inside I felt a sense of relief as I sighed and said, "So am I."

The End

Epilogue

2016: Nothing Lasts Forever

Gone are the days of misery. Don't get me wrong. Certainly not everything in my life is perfect. But a while ago I started to understand the well-known "Footprints in the Sand" poem. Looking back at the most difficult times of my life, with the perspective of time I realized I was never really alone.

Had I not been intercepted at Ninoy Aquino International Airport, it is unlikely that Maryl and I would have been reunited in just a month. My heart aches for mothers who leave their children to the care of other family members to come to the United States for the reasons why I did. What's ironic about this is that they often end up working as a nanny caring for other people's children. Most of them will work multiple jobs and some as domestic helpers, despite their college degrees. What saddens me the most is that some of these children are left with feelings of abandonment and wind up hating their parents for leaving them in the Philippines.

I now believe the red truck that came to my rescue from my abductor was an angel. I know God protected Maryl from my reckless driving when I wrecked my car. The car was totaled in the back, where she would normally sit, while the front seat window had not even a crack. Yet this was the first time I said yes to her request to sit in the front.

As for my mom and dad, I can now say that they both love me the best they know how. And it is sufficient. I have found a peaceful place in my heart in my relationship with both of them. My dad makes an effort to reach out to my sister and me. I think it's funny that he reaches out to me more when he's sick or in need of surgery. He seems to think I've got more favor "up there," as he puts it. Even when I tell him God helps everyone who believes no matter that person's current state of belief, my dad still says, "No, you do it." Sometimes, when it's just the two of us, I see his vulnerability. It is during these times when I get a glimpse of what his childhood must have been like. I realize that he, too, had it rough.

My mom is now living in the United States with my sister. I can only imagine the difficulty she must face daily to fight for her sobriety. I am most certain that some days it's a breeze, but other days it would be so much easier to reach for that bottle. I have learned to accept and understand that alcoholism is a disease. I have learned to hate the disease but not the alcoholic. She and I have had a few conversations about her past. My heart ached when she talked about raising my sister and me while she was still a teenager (17 years old). She told me how she would have to carry my sister on her back while she pushed a self-improvised swing to put me to sleep, because my sister and I were only 11 months apart. My mom described how one of her sisters-in-law would ask her to clean the house by mopping the floor with her bare hands—without paying her. That sister-in-law felt that my dad and mom living in their mother's basement was more than enough payment. I remember Grandma Annie telling me that she had to hide that she was giving my parents food because that sister-in-law didn't think it was right to do so.

My daughter Mary decided to drop her baby name Maryl during junior high. She went on to marry her childhood high school sweetheart. They now have two wonderful boys. Although Mary received her college degree, she decided to stay home to raise their children. I believe it was an excellent choice. But her decision had nothing to do with what I thought. I think she wanted to make sure her children would have what she never had—a mother who wasn't bombarded with worries and stress. When I look at her life, I am in awe of what God has done for us. I see Mary and her life as God's redemption from all my past hurt and pain because I made the decision to allow Him back into my life. Mary has everything I never had and then some. I have the joy of seeing the happiness in my grandchildren's lives. Mary is an exceptional mother. I often tell her, I would love to be one of her children. She is also a wonderful wife. She and her husband enjoy a great friendship, which is the basis of their love for one another. Together, they have created a special life.

As for me, I have been married for the past 21 years to the man

I married when Mary was 9½ years old. It would take another book to talk about my marriage because it would take too long to describe our challenges and struggles and the very difficult time of adjustment we both have had to work through. We have experienced pain together to survive. My marriage is not free of imperfections. But the saving grace of it all is our commitment to one another. We both will do whatever we need to do to push through, to see it through, and to make it no matter what it takes. Our love for one another goes very deep because it is bound by our understanding of God's love and by our friendship.

My marriage is probably one of the greatest challenges in which I have had to learn, grow, and conquer. I never knew what it was like to be married until I had to do it myself. My marriage and its struggles taught me to never judge anyone who has ever been divorced or is contemplating divorce. These real-life struggles also have helped me realize that feelings of love may come and go, but it is the decided-upon commitment that makes two people stay. It is safe for me to say that my husband and I work very hard at our relationship to stay together, to stay strong, and to not allow anything or anyone to ruin and destroy what we both work for. I feel very fortunate to admit that I never really knew what love was until I fell in love with my husband.

For all of this, I will forever be grateful to my God, who continues to heal me, sustain me, and show me what it truly means to love and be loved.

For Love Is the Greatest ...

❦

"Love is patient and kind. Love is not jealous or boastful or proud or rude. It does not demand its own way. It is not irritable, and it keeps no record of being wronged. It does not rejoice about injustice but rejoices whenever the truth wins out. Love never gives up, never loses faith, is always hopeful, and endures through every circumstance" (1 Corinthians 13:4–7, NLT).